The Twenty-six Qualities of a Devotee

Vaiṣṇava Behavior

The Twenty-six Qualities of a Devotee

Satsvarūpa dāsa Goswami

GN Press, Inc.

Persons interested in the subject matter of this book are invited to correspond with our secretary, c/o GN Press, Inc., PO Box 445, La Crosse, FL 32658 or please visit our web site at: www.gnpress.org.

GN Press gratefully acknowledges the BBT for the use of verses and purports from Śrīla Prabhupāda's books. All such verses and purports are © BBT.

Library of Congress In Publication Data:

Gosvāmī, Satsvarūpa Dāsa

Vaiṣṇava Behavior.

1. International Society for Krishna Consciousness. 2. Religious life (Vaiṣṇavism) I. Title.

BL1285.852.G67 1984 294.5'448 83-25447
ISBN 0-911233-18-0

Cover design: Madana-mohana dāsa

Contents

Vaiṣṇava Behavior

Preface

FIVE HUNDRED YEARS AGO, under the personal direction of Lord Caitanya, Sanātana Gosvāmī wrote all about Vaiṣṇava behavior in *Hari-bhakti-vilāsa,* and Śrīla Rūpa Gosvāmī wrote *Bhakti-rasāmṛta-sindhu.* In modern times, His Divine Grace A. C. Bhaktivedanta Swami Prabhupāda has given us the essence of Vaiṣṇava behavior throughout his writings, especially *The Nectar of Devotion* and *The Nectar of Instruction.* And Śrīla Prabhupāda's personal activities exemplified the highest standard of Vaiṣṇava behavior. Why then, should I write more about Vaiṣṇava behavior?

One reason is for my own purification; another is for others' purification. Because I am writing under orders from my spiritual master, Śrila Prabhupāda, my readers will receive authorized teachings about Lord Kṛṣṇa; and faithful hearing of such teachings will help them on the path back to Godhead. Certainly, as the Age of Kali worsens, the need for Kṛṣṇa conscious literature increases. In this age a person has almost no chance of rising to the standard of Vaiṣṇava (or even human) behaviour. Most people, totally disregarding basic laws for humanity as directed in the genuine scriptures and exemplified in the lives of saintly persons, are behaving even worse than the animals. Blind, materialistic leaders guide the blind masses, and everyone is falling in to the ditch of repeated birth and death. Therefore, we need authorized, Kṛṣṇa conscious books to offset the propaganda of nescience.

Devotees have requested me to write about Vaiṣṇava behavior and etiquette. They see the need not only to inform the nondevotees but to remind the members of the Kṛṣṇa consciousness movement. As the International Society for Krishna Consciousness (ISKCON) continues to expand all over the world, it is imperative that the members represent this movement rightly by exemplary behavior. If devotees are not saintly in their behavior, their preaching will ultimately be ineffective. A rebellious or ill-behaved disciple certainly brings disrepute to his spiritual master and becomes unnecessarily blasphemous to the holy name of Kṛṣṇa.

Even academic scholars who study the Kṛṣṇa consciousness movement understand the prime importance of example in the devotees' lives. Dr. Larry Shinn of Oberlin College was one of several professors interviewed by Stephen J. Gelberg in the book *Hare Krishna, Hare Krishna*. When Dr. Shinn was asked, "From your point of view, what are ISKCON's chances of survival as a religious institution?" he replied as follows:

> I think the movement will fare well precisely to the extent that the leaders adhere to the spiritual practices taught by Prabhupāda and to the extent that they have achieved the kinds of levels of spiritual advancement that come with those practices.

Shrivatsa Goswami of the Rādhā-rāmaṇa temple in Vṛndāvana said much the same thing when asked about the authenticity of the members of ISKCON: "The integrity, the sincerity, and the faithfulness of the devotees is the only proof—and sufficient proof—of its (ISKCON's) authenticity."

With these important facts in mind I am attempting to write a book on Vaiṣṇava behavior. When Lord Caitanya asked Sanātana Gosvāmī to write, Sanātana replied "I am a low-born person. I have no knowledge of good behavior. How is it possible for me to write authorized directions about Vaiṣṇava activities?" But Lord Caitanya assured him, "Whatever you want to do, you will be able to do correctly by Lord Kṛṣṇa's favor. He will manifest the real purport." My own assurance in daring to present a book on correct Vaiṣṇava behavior is that I am drawing everything from the purports of His Divine Grace A. C. Bhaktivedanta Swami Prabhupāda and acting on his instructions as a servant within the Kṛṣṇa consciousness movement. I pray to always keep myself in line so that my example doesn't discredit the valuable descriptions I have gathered here from Prabhupāda's books, letters, and teachings.

—SDG

Introduction

WHILE TOURING INDIA as a *sannyāsī,* Śrī Caitanya Mahāprabhu became ecstatic when he met a certain *brāhmaṇa* at the birthplace of Lord Kṛṣṇa in Mathurā. The *brāhmaṇa* was a disciple of Mādhavendra Purī, whom Lord Caitanya knew to be a highly advanced pure devotee of Rādhā-Kṛṣṇa. (Mādhavendra Purī was also the spiritual master of Īśvara Purī, Lord Caitanya's *guru.*) Lord Caitanya and the *brāhmaṇa* spontaneously danced and embraced, crying out, "Chant the holy names of Hari and Kṛṣṇa!" And they both began praising Mādhavendra Purī's pure love of God. Then Lord Caitanya Mahāprabhu utter these highly important words:

dharma-sthāpana-hetu sādhura vyavahāra
purī-gosāñira ye ācaraṇa, sei dharma sāra

> A devotee's behavior establishes the true purpose of religious principles. The behavior of Mādhavendra Purī Gosvāmī is the essence of such religious principles.
>
> —Cc. *Madhya* 17.185

In his purport to this verse, Śrīla Prabhupāda describes many kinds of persons who are not *mahājanas* (exemplary authorities), even though they may be great leaders in certain spheres of influence. "For the conditioned soul busy in sense gratification," writes Śrīla

Prabhupāda, "a *mahājana* is recognized according to the proportion of sense gratification he offers." Prabhupāda goes on to mention nondevotional *yogīs*, atheistic philosophers, demons like Hiraṇyakaśipu, anthropologists like Darwin, statesmen, and others whom foolish people consider to be exemplary leaders. But amidst the confusion of contending followers and their heroes, how can the real truth be established?

> A man covered by illusion cannot understand the proper way; therefore, Śrī Caitanya Mahāprabhu says: *dharma-sthāpana-hetu sādhura vyavahāra.* "The behavior of a devotee is the criterion for all other behavior." Śrī Caitanya Mahāprabhu Himself followed the devotional principles and taught others to follow them.
>
> —Cc. *Madhya* 17.185, purport

People who stubbornly refuse to accept transcendental knowledge and who therefore accept the body and mind as the real self will continue to follow false *mahājanas* or promises for a happiness that is flickering and destructable. Many who set out in search of truth will also be distracted by *māyā* or misled by cheaters in the guise of *mahājanas.* But those who persist will find the truth in the lives of the genuine *mahājanas.* "Śrī Mādhavendra Purī was a real *mahājana,*" writes Śrīla Prabhupāda, "because he understood the Absolute Truth properly and throughout his life behaved like a pure devotee."

In discussing with the *brāhmaṇa* at Mathurā, Lord Caitanya quoted from the *Mahābhārata,* establishing the exclusive importance of a devotee's behavior:

tarko 'prātiṣṭha srutayo vibinna
nāsāv ṛṣir yasya mataṁ na bhinnam
dharmasya tattvaṁ nihitaṁ guhāyaṁ
mahājano yena gataḥ sa panthaḥ

> Śrī Caitanya Mahāprabhu continued, "Dry arguments are inconclusive. A great personality whose opinion does not differ from others is not considered a great sage. Simply by studying the Vedas, which are variegated, one cannot come to the right path by which religious principles are understood. The solid truth of religious principles is hidden in the heart of an unadulterated, self-realized person. Consequently, as the *śastras* confirm, one should accept whatever progressive path the mahājanas advocate.
>
> —*Mahābhārata, Vana-parva* 313.117
> (as quoted in Cc. *Madhya* 17.186)

This verse has several remarkable features. One point is that the Absolute Truth cannot be learned directly from the scriptures. The *Vedas* are perfect; they are so voluminous and yet their meanings so grave that an ordinary person cannot understand them. Also, the scriptures sometimes appear contradictory. Because of this difficulty, the sages at Naimiṣāraṇya requested Sūta Gosvāmī to select from the many available scriptures and present the essence of religious principles.

Another difficulty is that one may read the scriptures and grasp them theoretically but conclude that the perfection of spiritual life cannot actually be found within this world. Still another problem is that one may receive a distorted or interpreted version of scriptural teachings from various sages, *yogīs*, or *swamis*. But from the above verse from the *Mahābhārata* we learn that a *muni*, or sage, does not become well-known unless he deliberately fashions a new interpretation on the truth.

This is similar to the tradition of Western philosophy, where a thinker is recognized for contradicting or outdoing the speculations of previous philosophers. If one thinks he can find the truth by following a certain speculative philosopher, he may find that in the future another philosopher will find faults in the system of the presently admired philosopher. Thus one's search for the truth will remain always inconclusive. "The solid truth of religious principles is hidden in the heart of an unadulterated, self-realized person." From the pure devotee you can directly get all the benefits of religious principles, which may not be available from all other sources combined. Everything becomes as clear as sunlight by the effulgent activities and words of the genuine *mahājana*.

It is also the compassionate *mahājana's* nature to give instructions so that we can better follow his example; and these instructions may include extensive rules of behavior. In the Kṛṣṇa consciousness movement, His Divine Grace Śrīla Prabhupāda instituted both basic and advanced rules. The most basic is that one should chant the Hare Kṛṣṇa *mantra* at least sixteen rounds a day and should avoid illicit sex, intoxication, gambling, and meat-eating. Whoever sincerely accepts this behavior can elevate himself beyond sinful life to the standard of eternal devotional service to Lord Kṛṣṇa.

The sublime value of devotional service cannot be realized by merely theoretical acceptance. This is explained by Śrīla Prabhupāda in *The Nectar of Devotion*:

> The particular word used by Śrīla Rūpa Gosvāmī in this connection is *anuśīlana,* or cultivation by following the predecessor teachers (*ācāryas*). As soon as we say "cultivation," we must refer to activity. Without activity, consciousness alone cannot help us.

The *siddhānta,* or conclusion, of Lord Caitanya's words to the *brāhmaṇa* is that *religious truth is manifested preeminently in the behavior of a pure devotee.* An aspirant for spiritual life must therefore find out such an exemplary devotee, accept him as his spiritual master, and follow his instructions with great faith.

Just as religious principles are established by the behavior of a pure Vaiṣṇava, so it is conversely true that the repute of religion is marred by the ill behavior of someone who claims to be a Vaiṣṇava.

Śrīla Prabhupāda explains that the leaders of society must protect themselves as well as their followers from the vices of Kali-yuga.

> The progressive religionists and those who are responsible human beings or those who do not want to spoil their valuable human lives should refrain from all the principles of irreligiosity, especially illicit connection with women. If a *brāhmaṇa* is not truthful, all his claims as a *brāhmaṇa* at once becomes null and void. If a *sannyāsī* is illicitly connected with women, all his claims as a *sannyāsī* at once become false. Similarly, if the king and the public leader are unnecessarily proud or habituated to drinking or smoking, certainly they become disqualified to discharge public welfare activities. Truthfulness is the basic principle for all religions. The four leaders of the human society, namely the *sannyāsīs,* the *brāhmaṇa,* the king and the public leader, must be tested crucially by their character and qualifications. Before one can be accepted as a spiritual or material master of society, he must be tested by the above-mentioned criteria of character. Such public leaders may be less qualified in academic qualifications, but it is necessary primarily that they be free from the contamination of the four disqualifications, namely gambling, drinking, prostitution, and animal slaughter.
>
> —*Bhāg.* 1.17.41

Again, behavior is the criterion, and since the devotee is the standard for the most important part of life—spiritual advancement—his misbehavior is the greatest disservice to society. There are priests and rabbis and ministers and *swamis* who may appear to hold leadership within their sects, but the real test of leadership is something different from political control or maintaining many followers. To be a real devotee in Kṛṣṇa consciousness, one has to behave as a devotee according to the standards of Vaiṣṇava behavior.

Hypocrisy is dishonesty, and according to Śrīla Prabhupāda's purport, without honesty there is no question of spiritual life: "Truthfulness is the basic principle for all religions." When religionists misbehave, the spread of God consciousness is checked. For example, a basic principle in Kṛṣṇa consciousness is that the student must hear from authority. This is an all-important philosophical point. Not by sense perception or by theorizing, but only by hearing from authority can one receive information from the Absolute Truth, beyond the range of the imperfect senses and mind.

Agnostic critics try to argue that such hearing is dogmatic, but the Viasṇavas reply that *all* learning requires one to hear from an authority. In the case of Vedic knowledge, the authority is the Supreme Personality of Godhead, and we hear through His direct representatives in disciplic succession, bona fide *gurus* and *sādhus*. But if the *gurus* and *sādhus* behave hypocritically, then their teaching cannot be accepted as a transparent via medium, and the whole epistemological system of receiving the truth breaks down. Of course, there are always pure devotees present, even when hypocrites crowd the scene, as in Kali-yuga. But the hypocritical teachers tend to give the impression that all authorities are charlatans. The misbehaving *brahmacārī, gṛhastha,* or *sannyāsī* hurst the cause of religion for all people, since the bad example breeds cynicism.

The *Śrīmad-Bhāgavatam* relates how King Indra disguised himself as a *sannyāsī* to interrupt the sacrificial performances of Mahārāja Pṛthu. Previous to that, the demon Rāvaṇa had disguised himself as a saintly mendicant to kidnap Sītā, the chaste wife of Lord Rāmacandra. Śrīla Prabhupāda comments that the government's duty is to stop fraudulent religious practices. But governments of today cannot ascertain what is religion or irreligion. "Because of this," Śrīla Prabhupāda writes, "citizens are generally becoming uninterested in spiritual advancement. Thus the situation deteriorates to such an extent that human society becomes hellish. (*Bhāg.* 4.19.26, purport)

"Caesar's wife should be above suspicion," Śrīla Prabhupāda used to quote, meaning that a devotee must be exemplary. If people suspect that a representative of God is cheating on the very principles he is supposed to be upholding, then how can they hear him with faith? If a man advises others not to smoke cigarettes but he himself smokes, of what value are his words?

In teaching his disciples, Jesus Christ sternly ordered them to restrict their behavior if they wished to be considered Christians.

> You are the salt of the earth; but if salt has lost its taste, how shall its saltness be restored? It is no longer good for anything except to be thrown out and trodden underfoot by men.
>
> Whoever then relaxes one of the least of these commandments and teaches men so, shall be called least in

the kingdom of heaven; but he who does them and teaches them shall be called great in the kingdom of heaven.

—*Matthew* 5.13 & 19

Enemies of Kṛṣṇa consciousness and media sensationalists make false propaganda about the devotees, and that can be harmful to the spreading of religious principles. But despite the bigotry and the scare stories from apostates, people will be intestered to find out for themselves what the devotees are actually like. Persecution may come and go, but the real behavior of the devotees will create a lasting impression. If the behavior is according to Vaiṣṇava principles, then the impression will be favorable, at least for those who are sincere. In a letter to a disciple in India, Śrīla Prabhupāda expressed confidence that visitors to the temple would be impressed if the devotional activities were in order.

> As soon as they will see our activities, they will be very much pleased. . . Let them come in the evening, see kirtana, take prasada, and liberally contribute. They will fell relieved to contribute to such a good cause.
>
> —Letter, September 3, 1974 to Girirāja dāsa

Lord Kṛṣṇa, the Supreme Personality of Godhead, is never deceived for a minute. He knows His sincere devotees are following His instructions, and He always protects them. And He also knows who is hypocritical. Since success in devotional service is based on pleasing Lord Kṛṣṇa and His representative, and since Kṛṣṇa is all-knowing, a hypocrite cannot advance spiritually. But for one who is fully surrendered to Kṛṣṇa, there is no fear or failure: "O son of Kuntī, declare it boldly that My devotee never perishes."

Acting as the representative of Kṛṣṇa, Śrīla Prabhupāda guided his disciples to take shelter of the rules and regulations of Vaiṣṇava behavior as the sure means to victory.

> My only anxiety is to guide you. . . The main guidance is that all of us should remain spiritually strong by chanting the minimum number of rounds and following the rules and regulations. The GBC [Governing Body Commission of ISKCON] should personally observe strictly all the rules and regulations and they should become the practical example to others. Then everything will be all right. Then there will be no fear of being victimized by maya.
>
> —Letter, September 5, 1974 to Bali-mardana dāsa

Vaiṣṇava Behavior contains three chapters. Chapter One concerns the relationship of preaching to behavior. Chapter Two discusses four kinds of personal relationships a devotee develops according to Vaiṣṇava principles. Chapter Three extensively enumerates principles and rules of behavior that govern devotees in the Kṛṣṇa consciousness movement.

I have tried to avoid presenting my own opinions. Throughout the book I have advocated the conclusion as spoken by Lord Caitanya to the *brāhmaṇa* at Mathurā: "A devotee's behavior establishes the true purpose of religious principles." I find that His Divine Grace Śrīla Prabhupāda is also strongly advocating this conclusion, just as he stated in a letter to one of his disciples:

> I am seeing more and more that my senior disciples must take an active role in continuing the high standard of purity which has been established in our Vaisnava line. In your traveling from center to center, you

must be very careful to see that the leaders are observing the principles of chanting 16 rounds, rising early for Mangala Arati, participating in the morning and evening classes, observing the four regulative principles, etc. and if there is any deviation from this standard then it is the responsibility of you and the local GBC representative to rectify it immediately. Within these Vaisnava standards which I have put forward lies the spiritual strength of our movement.

—Letter, February 16, 1973 to Sudāmā dāsa

Preaching and Behavior

BETWEEN PREACHING and behavior there exists a dynamic tension. This is expressed in Sanātana Gosvāmī's praise of Haridāsa Ṭhākura.

> Some behave well but do not preach the cult of Kṛṣṇa consciousness, whereas others preach but do not behave properly.
>
> You simultaneously perform both duties in relation to the holy name by your personal behavior and your preaching. Therefore you are the spiritual master of the entire world for you are the most advanced devotee in the world.

Śrīla Prabhupāda confirms that his own followers also must preach and behave in an exemplary way:

> The qualifications expressed in this connection are that one must act according to the scriptural injunctions and at the same time preach...the members of the Kṛṣṇa consciousness movement chant a minimum sixteen rounds a day, which can be done without difficulty, and at the same time they must preach the cult of Caitanya Mahāprabhu according to the gospel of *Bhagavad-gītā As It Is*. One who does so is quite fit to become a spiritual master for the entire world.
>
> —Cc. *Antya* 4.102–103

The word *preaching* refers to many things. Preaching means printing and distributing Kṛṣṇa conscious literature. It means holding festivals like Ratha-yātrā and utilizing "cultural weapons," including art and theater, to inform the public about the teachings of the *Bhagavad-gītā.* Preaching means meeting people on the street, in the college classroom, and in the home and telling them about Kṛṣṇa. It means engaging people at ISKCON temples and farm communities. It means showing families how they can practice *bhakti-yoga* in their homes and how they can serve Lord Kṛṣṇa through their occupation. Preaching means raising and educating children for returning to the spiritual world. Preaching enters into all spheres of life, including social action, economics, and politics. And wherever the preacher goes, he glorifies the Supreme Personality of Godhead.

Rūpa Gosvāmī has explained that a devotee should never renounce anything that can be used in the service of Kṛṣṇa. Even material objects like telephones, computers, jet planes, and automobiles may be used to broadcast Kṛṣṇa's message. And when used in pure devotional service, any material object becomes a spiritualized instrument. For distributing Kṛṣṇa consciousness there should be no restriction. Furthermore, devotional service is applicable in any country and for any person, in any condition of life.

We have been stressing exemplary behavior, yet it cannot be done in a vacuum—it cannot be done without preaching. In fact, preaching activities are the essence of right behavior for a Vaiṣṇava. Nārada Muni is an exemplary preacher, and Śrīla Prabhupāda recommends that all devotees follow in Nārada's footsteps: "Their only business is to chant and remember the holy name, fame and pastimes of the Lord and, according to personal capacity, to distribute the message for others welfare without motive of material gain." (*Bhāg.* 1.6.26, purport)

Bhaktisiddhānta Sarasvatī Ṭhākura has derided solitary chanting as a king of cheating performed to attain name and fame. Similarly, if one simply engages in temple worship but doesn't see to the welfare of the masses, he is on the lowest rung of devotional service. A devotee should not retire to the forest in search of the ideal place for executing Vaiṣṇava behavior. Rather, he should stay in the cities and offer people the chance to go back to Godhead. The *Śrīmad-Bhāgavatam* states that if a *brāhmana* neglects those who are in want of Kṛṣṇa consciousness, that *brāhmana's* spiritual knowledge will diminish, "just as water kept in a cracked pot leaks out." (*Bhāg*. 4.14.41)

Lord Caitanya also expected His direct followers to do their daily share of preaching, indicating that preaching is not optional—it is a must.

> The devotees of Lord Caitanya must preach Kṛṣṇa consciousness in every village and town in the world. That will satisfy the Lord. It is not that one should act whimsically for his own personal satisfaction. This order comes down through the *paramparā* system, and the spiritual master presents these orders to the disciple so that he can spread the message of Śrī Caitanya Mahāprabhu. It is the duty of every disciple to carry out the order of the bona fide spiritual master and spread Lord Caitanya's message all over the world.
>
> —Cc. *Madhya* 16.64, purport

Therefore, whenever we stress good behavior for the Vaiṣṇava, it should be understood that the Vaiṣṇava is a preacher. "Every devotee should be very enthusiastic," writes Prabhupāda, "not only in performing his daily rituals of devotional service, but in trying to preach the cult peacefully by following in the footsteps of Lord Caitanya. If he is not superficially successful in such an attempt, he should not be deterred from the discharge of his duty." (*Bhāg*. 2.8.21, purport)

If a devotee tries to avoid preaching, he cannot become spiritually advance. Indeed, Śrīla Bhaktivinoda Ṭhākura has said that the position of a Vaiṣṇava can be tested by seeing how good a touchstone he is—that is, by seeing how many Vaiṣṇavas he has made during his life.

Nevertheless, we should not consider the rules and regulations of Vaiṣṇava behavior to be some mere ritual or formality. "The first preaching work," Śrīla Prabhupāda wrote in a letter, "is that you yourself should become an ideal devotee." (April 23, 1974 to Niranjana dāsa) This is also express by Lord Caitanya: *āpani ācari' bhakti śikhāimu sābre.* "First become perfect and then preach." The physician has to heal himself before he goes forward to help others.

> Go on preaching with vigorous enthusiasm, and increase your program for bringing new men to live in Kṛṣṇa consciousness.
>
> You yourself must be ideal in following the rules and regulations, rising early, and restricting eating and sleeping. The less a person is concerned with material enjoyment such as eating, sex, and sleeping, the more he is spiritually advanced. If the "devotee" himself lives like a hog or dog, how can he preach?
>
> —Letter, January 26, 1977 to Danavir dāsa

Only an immature preacher thinks that he can maintain enthusiasm for his outgoing service while at the same time not pay strict attention to the rules and regulations. In an Eleventh Canto purport, Hridayānanda Mahārāja writes:

> One who has achieved the shelter of the Lord's holy name and is totally engaged in the attempt to serve the Lord should be considered to be on the platform of *bhajana,* even though his external activities may sometimes be less strict than those of the neophyte engaged in *arcana.* The apparent lack of strictness, however, refers to laxity, not on the basic principles of sane behavior and renunciation of sense gratification, but rather in the detail of Vaiṣṇava ceremonies.
>
> —*Bhāg.* 11.2.46

Māyā is undoubtedly very strong, and preachers have to be vigilant like soldiers in a fortress. By keeping all activities Kṛṣṇa conscious, a preacher will not allow *māyā* to enter. Śrīla Bhaktisiddhānta Sarasvatī used to say that a preacher has to have life; he cannot be a dead man. Vital spiritual life depends on strict Vaiṣṇava behavior. "Preaching work is strong," wrote Prabhupāda to a temple leader in 1972, "if our routine work is strong. Never neglect our regular program and that will be your success."

Kṛṣṇa consciousness cannot be effectively spread to every town and village merely by purchasing many vans and training devotees to drive them. Delivering Kṛṣṇa consciousness is a far greater task than that performed by companies like United Parcel Service. The devotee is similar to the mailman in that he delivers the message of Kṛṣṇa without adulteration, but to be a representative of Kṛṣṇa requires deep conviction and purity. Śrīla Prabhupāda criticized devotees for going out to sell Kṛṣṇa conscious books without knowing the philosophy in the books.

> We want to create pure devotees so that other people will benefit by their association . . . To make a show of

> devotional service will not help one. One must be a pure devotee following the pure devotional process . . . If a preacher behaves properly in devotional service, he will be able to convert others. Otherwise, his preaching will have no effect.
>
> —Cc. *Madhya* 24.98, purport

To think that a Vaiṣṇava can preach and yet remain ignorant of the Vaiṣṇava philosophy or disregard the standard principles of Vaiṣṇava behavior is ludicrous. As stated in the *Bhakti-rasāmṛta-sindhu*:

śruti smṛti purānādi,
pañcarātra-vidhiṁ vina,
aikāntikī harer bhaktir
utpātāyaiva kalpate

> Devotional service performed without reference to the authorized scriptures simply creates a disturbance in society.

BEHAVIOR IN PREACHING

A Devotee is a Gentleman

When a television interviewer asked Śrīla Prabhupāda by what behavior one could recognize a true follower of Kṛṣṇa consciousness, Śrīla Prabhupāda replied, "He'd be the perfect gentleman, that's all." And in translating the *Bhagavad-gītā* verses listing eighteen items of knowledge (Bg. 13.8–12), Śrīla Prabhupāda translates the word *amānitvam* as, "one should himself become a perfect gentleman and learn to give proper respect to others." Although in ordinary usage the word *gentleman* may refer to a man of wealth and aristocracy, we use it here to describe a devotee's high standard of honorable and considerate behavior. The polite and humble behavior of a devotee can be appreciated even by the nondevotee. A devotee is not arrogant, boorish, or inconsiderate of others.

In the *Śrīmad-Bhāgavatam* 1.5.29, Nārada Muni explains that he was favored by the Vaiṣṇavas because, "I was gentle in behavior, and all my sins were eradicated in their service." Commenting on this verse, Śrīla Prabhupāda remarks, "One should not be misled by a pseudodevotee. He himself must be plain and gentle to receive the instructions of such a pure devotee."

In His own preaching Lord Caitanya Mahāprabhu displayed cool-headed, polite behavior, even when engaged in debate. On one occasion he demonstrated extraordinary humility and tolerance by sitting silently for seven days while Sārvabhauma Bhaṭṭācārya lectured to Him on *Vedānta Sūtra*. Only when the Bhaṭṭācārya inquired of His silence did the Lord begin his opposition to the Māyāvāda interpretation of *Vedānta*. When Lord Caitanya came into the company of Māyāvādi *sannyāsīs* at Benares, He sat down humbly at the doorway until the chief *sannyāsī*, Prakāśānanda Sarasvatī, personally came to invite Him inside. And on subsequent visits to Benares, Lord Caitanya displayed similar gentleness and humility.

> When people came to Śrī Caitanya Mahāprabhu to discuss the principles of various scriptures, the Lord defeated their false conclusions and established the predominance of devotional service to the Lord. With logic and argument he very politely changed their minds.
>
> —Cc. *Madhya* 25.20

As a youth Lord Caitanya soundly defeated a Kāshmīrī *paṇḍita* in debate. But when Lord Caitanya's students began to laugh at the *paṇḍita*, Lord Caitanya silenced them and treated His opponent with honor. When Lord Caitanya started a civil disobedience *kīrtana* against the Kazi's order in Navadvīpa, He certainly defied the law, but nonviolently. "If we become violent in every case," comments Śrīla Prabhupāda, "it will be difficult for us to manage our affairs. We should therefore follow in the footsteps of Lord Caitanya Mahāprabhu, who disobeyed the order of Chand Kazi but subdued him with reason and argument." (Cc. *Adi* 17.130, purport) Although Lord Caitanya led 100,000 men in *kīrtana* to the Kazi's residence, on arriving there, He discussed peacefully with the Kazi, treating him like an honorable elder. Śrīla Prabhupāda comments, "In pushing on our *saṅkīrtana* movement of Kṛṣṇa consciousness, we might have to face difficult days, but we should always follow in the footsteps of Śrī Caitanya Mahāprabhu and do the needful according to the time and circumstances." (Cc. *Adi* 17.144, purport)

The scriptures advise, *satyaṁ bruyāt priyaṁ bruyāt*: "In this material world only palatable truths should be spoken. Unpalatable truths should be carefully avoided." Prabhupāda discussed this intricately in his correspondence with Sumati Morarjee concerning a controversy regarding Lord Caitanya and Vallabhācārya. Sumati Morarjee was a follower of Vallabhācārya, and she felt offended when she read in a *Back to Godhead* magazine that Lord Caitanya had criticized Vallabhācārya, comparing him in one instance to an unfaithful wife. Śrīla Prabhupāda apologized. "It is certainly unpleasant," he wrote, "but the officers who publish the magazine do not know *satyaṁ bruyāt priyaṁ bruyāt.*"

Śrīla Prabhupāda went on to say that the cause of Lord Caitanya's agitation was much the same as Mrs. Morarjee's. "As you are irritated by the criticism of Sri

Vallabhācārya," Śrīla Prabhupāda wrote, "similarly Sri Caitanya Mahaprabhu was also agitated when Vallabhacarya criticized Sridhara Svami." Prabhupāda further explained that all the Vaiṣṇava *ācāryas* honor Śrīdhara Svāmī as the first commentator on the *Śrīmad-Bhāgavatam.* Vallabhācārya claimed that his own commentary on *Śrīmad-Bhāgavatam* was superior; he found Śrīdhara Svāmī's unacceptable. In response to this, Lord Caitanya criticized Vallabhācārya. Otherwise, Śrīla Prabhupāda explained, Lord Caitanya and Vallabhācārya were friends, and their argument could be compared to the argument of two lawyers in the courtroom; after the debate they are again friends. Śrīla Prabhupāda's concluding remarks in this letter serve as a guide for Vaiṣṇava etiquette in dealing with delicate controversial points.

> Devotees always humbly offer respect to everyone, but when there is discussion on a point of *sastra,* they do not observe the usual etiquette, *satyam bruyat priyam bruyat.* They speak only the *satyam,* although it may not necessarily be *priyam.*
>
> —Letter, August 9, 1976 to Sumati Morarjee

We may further note that although Śrīla Prabhupāda asserted the *satyaṁ* (truth) to Mrs. Morarjee without compromise, his behavior was still *priyaṁ* (palatable).

Even if the devotee speaks politely, dresses neatly, and acts with all consideration, he will be rejected by many materialistic men. Once in 1968, Śrīla Prabhupāda sent a simple *brahmacāri* to Florida, where a Mr. Fugate claimed to be interested in hearing about *bhakti-yoga.* After the *brahmacāri* visited, Mr. Fugate wrote back that he was not impressed with the representative of Kṛṣṇa consciousness. Prabhupāda responded with compassion and consideration, both for his disciple and for Mr. Fugate. "Anyway," wrote Śrīla Prabhupāda, "please try to deal with him [Mr. Fugate] softly, because he has got some tendency for spiritual upliftment of his life, but he is misguided or without any knowledge in the line." Prabhupāda repeated the Sanskrit proverb that one should speak only palatable truth. "This is a social convention," wrote Prabhupāda, "and is not applicable to a person who is preaching the Absolute Truth. The Absolute Truth is not dependent on material pleasure or displeasure."

All things considered, a devotee should try his best to act as a Vaiṣṇava lady or gentleman and behave politely, as did Lord Caitanya Mahāprabhu. If in the course of sincerely delivering the Absolute Truth, the nondevotees regard us as unimpressive, then that will not disturb us. A devotee has to please his spiritual master and Kṛṣṇa, and then everything is complete, even if the world finds him lacking.

When Śrīla Prabhupāda refers to the devotee as a gentleman, he generally means that a devotee avoids the abominable activities of illicit sex, meat-eating, intoxication, and gambling. The so-called ladies and gentlemen of the world who dress well and speak with culture yet eat slaughtered animals and engage in illicit activities are actually more like beasts than humans. For Vaiṣṇava behavior, the all-important etiquette is to staunchly follow the regulative principles and the exemplary behavior of the *mahājanas*.

Vaiṣṇava Behavior in Different Relationships

IN THE ELEVENTH CANTO of *Śrīmad-Bhāgavatam* three classes of devotees are discussed: the most advance (*bhāgavata-uttama*), the intermediate (*madhyama-bhakta*), and the materialistic devotee (*prākṛta-bhakta*). Śrīla Prabhupāda informs us in *The Nectar of Instruction* that to preach one must act on the *madhyama-bhakta* platform. Because one on the topmost platform sees everything and everyone as perfectly situated within Śrī Kṛṣṇa, the Supreme Personality of Godhead, he doesn't distinguish between atheists and devotees. In this highest consciousness, he may remain absorbed in a trance of meditation upon the Supreme Lord, even while residing in the material world. But to preach as Lord Caitanya Mahāprabhu has ordered, a pure devotee must distinguish between the avowed atheists and the innocent, who can be effectively approached with Kṛṣṇa consciousness. Seeing these distinctions is the symptom of the intermediate devotee, as described in the *Śrīmad-Bhāgavatam*:

> An intermediate or second-class devotee, called *madhyama-adhikārī*, offers his love to the Supreme Personality of Godhead, is a sincere friend to all the devotees of the Lord, shows mercy to ignorant people who

are innocent, and disregards those who are envious of the Supreme Personality of Godhead.

—*Bhāg*. 11.2.46

It will be relevant, therefore, if we consider Vaiṣṇava behavior through the vision of the intermediate, *madhyama-bhakta*.

THE MADHYAMA-BHAKTA OFFERS HIS LOVE TO THE SUPREME PERSONALITY OF GODHEAD

Serving the Spiritual Master

Love of God begins by hearing about Him from His authorized representative, the Vaiṣṇava spiritual master. This is called *śravaṇa*. A devotee's relationship with God, therefore, begins with his relationship with God's representative, the spiritual master. The disciple understands his spiritual master to be sent by Kṛṣṇa to save him. And he understands that pleasing the spiritual master is the most important principle in spiritual life and is the secret of advancement.

All the Vaiṣṇava scriptures emphasize that one's relationship with Kṛṣṇa is realized through one's relationship with the *guru*. This is explained in *Gurv-aṣṭaka*, "Eight Prayers to the Spiritual Master," composed by Śrīla Viśvanātha Cakravartī Ṭhākura. Of this prayer, Viśvanātha Cakravartī writes, "One who, with great care and attention, loudly recites this beautiful prayer to the spiritual master during the *brāhma-muhūrta* obtain direct service to Kṛṣṇa, the Lord of Vṛndāvana, at the demise of his body."

By meditating on the verses of the *Gurv-aṣṭaka*, we shall enter the glories of the *guru*-disciple relationship.

1

> The spiritual master is receiving benediction from the ocean of mercy. Just as a cloud pours water on a forest fire to extinguish it, so the spiritual master delivers the materially afflicted world by extinguishing the blazing fire of material existence. I offer my respectful obeisances unto the lotus feet of such a spiritual master, who is an ocean of auspicious qualities.

In the beginning, the disciple may have only an inkling of the identity of his eternal spiritual master. But when that inkling becomes his heart's conviction, he understands that his spiritual master has come from Kṛṣṇa, the Supreme Personality of Godhead, and that his spiritual master can save him from the ocean of repeated birth and death.

It is the *guru* himself who has to teach this to us. Lord Caitanya explained to Rūpa Gosvāmī that the eternal spiritual souls are wandering throughout the universe, birth after birth. Only by the mercy of the spiritual master, sent by Kṛṣṇa, do we get the chance of eternal life in devotional service. The spiritual master offers this great blessing to us, and we have to hear it with faith. Only as we gradually understand our relationship with our spiritual master will we understand our real self and our relationship with God. All the knowledge available carried by the entire disciplic succession is available to us through our spiritual master. Therefore, Śrīla Viśvanātha Cakravartī Ṭhākura says that we should offer our respectful obeisances unto the lotus feet of our spiritual master.

When the Kṛṣṇa consciousness movement was barely beginning in the West, in 1968, a disciple wrote to Śrīla Prabhupāda and asked how he should offer his food to Kṛṣṇa. Śrīla Prabhupāda replied that the offering would be complete if the disciple simply offered the food to the spiritual master, who would then take charge of offering it to Kṛṣṇa.

> For offering prasadam simply prayers to the Spiritual Master is sufficient. The process is that everything is offered to the Spiritual Master, and the Spiritual Master is supposed to offer the same foodstuff to the Lord. When a thing is offered to the Spiritual Master, he immediately offers to the Lord. That is the system, and as we come by parampara system, it is our duty to go through the right channel—namely, first the Spiritual Master, then Lord Caitanya, and then Kṛṣṇa. So when we chant prayers, we do this, Bande ham Sri Guru . . . and gradually to the Goswamis, then to Lord Caitanya, and then to Radha Krishna. That is the praying system. But offering the prasadam to present everything before the Spiritual Master whose picture is also on the altar, means that the Spiritual Master will take care of offering the foodstuff to the Lord. Therefore simply by chanting the prayer to the Spiritual Master, everything will be complete.
>
> —Letter dated May 28, 1968

Before meeting the spiritual master, we are so covered by illusion that we don't even know we're suffering the pangs of birth and death. But he opens our eyes. Once we understand from him that we are in the ocean of *saṁsāra,* of repeated birth and death, we desire to get out, so we turn sincerely to him. He is the representative of Kṛṣṇa; if he accepts our service, then we are safe.

2

Chanting the holy name, dancing in ecstasy, singing, and playing musical instruments, the spiritual master is always gladdened by the *saṅkīrtana* movement of Lord Caitanya Mahāprabhu. Because he is relishing the mellows of pure devotion within his mind, sometimes his hair stands on end, he feels quivering in his body, and tears flow from his eyes like waves. I offer my respectful obeisances unto the lotus feet of such a spiritual master.

By Kṛṣṇa's grace, the spiritual master is an ecstatic devotee; he is always engladdened by the *saṅkīrtana* movement. Naturally, he engages his disciple in chanting the holy name, and dancing, singing, and playing musical instruments. Then the disciple also becomes ecstatic in the natural happiness of *kīrtana*. Except for the grace of the spiritual master, the disciple could never enter the *kīrtana-rasa. Sampradāya-vihīnā ye mantras te niṣpalā matāh*: "Unless you have received the *mantra* in disciplic succession from the spiritual master, it will not have the desired effect." The spiritual master is like a touchstone. He gives us the holy name, and if we chant the name with devotion, we realize our relationship with Kṛṣṇa.

Sometimes the spiritual master is with us in his personal form (*vapuḥ*), but more often not. Yet in either case, as we chant and dance in *kīrtana* under his instructions, our relationship with him will grow and improve. Lord Kṛṣṇa says that although He is not personally present in the heart of the *yogī*, or even in Vaikuṇtha, He is present wherever His pure devotees chant His name.

This is also true of the spiritual master; if we desire to be with him always and serve at his lotus feet, then just by chanting the Hare Kṛṣṇa *mantra* (in *kīrtana* or in *japa*) as he has instructed, we can experience his presence and approval. As we chant the holy name under the order of the spiritual master, we are always united with our Lord and His pure devotee.

As for the importance of *kīrtana,* Śrīla Prabhupāda has stated, "We should always remember the danger of *māyā's* influence and endeavor to save ourselves from her great power. We must, therefore, always merge in the transcendental mellow of *kīrtana-rasa,* for *kīrtana-rasa* is the safest situation within this material world."

3

> The spiritual master is always engaged in the temple worship of Śrī Śrī Rādhā and Kṛṣṇa. He also engages his disciples in such worship. They dress the Deities in beautiful clothes and ornaments, clean Their temple, and perform other similar worship of the Lord. I offer my respectful obeisances unto the lotus feet of such a spiritual master.

The spiritual master introduces us to our relationship with the Deity. He invites Rādhā and Kṛṣṇa to descend and he bathes and dresses Their forms before the eyes of his disciples. He demonstrates the principle of *utsāhā,* enthusiasm, because without enthusiasm the worship becomes like idol worship. After the spiritual master installs the Deity in the temple, it is up to the disciples to faithfully carry on the worship with enthusiasm.

> *Śrī-vigraha* is the *arcā,* or suitable worshipable form of the Lord, and the disciple should be engaged in worshiping the Deity regularly by *śṛṅgāra,* by proper decoration and dressing, as also by *mandira-mārjana,* the matter of cleansing the temple. The spiritual master teaches the neophyte devotee all these kindly and personally to help him gradually in the realization of the transcendental name, quality, form, etc., of the Lord.
>
> —*Bhāg.* 2.3.22, purport

Worship of the Deity in the temple, or any service to the spiritual master, must be done with an abiding sense of obedience. In the early stages of devotion obedience is important in our loving relationship with God, and it is formed in our relation to the *guru*. Out of obedience to the spiritual master, we rise early in the morning, just as if he were present before us turning on the light or ringing the bell to wake us. By his order we bathe, sit down to chant the *mahā-mantra*, and then enter the temple room to awaken the Deity and perform *maṅgala-ārati*. A sense of obedience is the primary motivating force when we are serving in the *sādhana* stage. Rūpa Gosvāmī describes *sādhana* as devotional activities performed under obligation, before one is actually motivated by spontaneous love. But that sense of obligation is based on love for the spiritual master. Because we cannot bear becoming disobedient to our spiritual master, we attend to our duties and find strength to not fall into sinful life.

To honor the spiritual master means to carry out his instructions word for word. When Lord Brahmā observed such a complete acceptance of his instructions by his son Kardama, he praised it as exemplary: "Sons ought to render service to their father, exactly to this extent. One should obey the command of his father or spiritual master with due deference, saying 'Yes, sir'" (*Bhāg*. 3.24.13)

Commenting on this verse, Śrīla Prabhupāda writes, "The son or disciple should accept the words of his spiritual master and father without hesitation. Whatever the father or the spiritual master order should be taken without argument: 'Yes.' There should be no instance in which the disciple or the son says, 'This is not correct. I cannot carry it out.' When he says that, he is fallen."

But if a disciple treats his relationship with the spiritual master as a mere formality, then he cannot advance or realize Kṛṣṇa consciousness. The *guru* is not like a family priest for performing ritual ceremonies, nor is he a figurehead appointed by the institution, without real presence in the heart and mind of the disciple. Rather the spiritual master is the center of the disciple's very being—"He is my lord, birth after birth."

4

> The spiritual master is always offering Kṛṣṇa four kinds of delicious food (analyzed as that which is licked, chewed, drunk, and sucked). When the spiritual master sees that the devotees are satisfied by eating *bhagavata-prasāda,* he is satisfied. I offer my respectful obeisances unto the lotus feet of such a spiritual master.

Honoring Kṛṣṇa's *prasādam* is a very important part of Kṛṣṇa consciousness. The spiritual master guides us here also, by accepting our prayers to Kṛṣṇa and by offering us from his own hand the Lord's remnants. The exchange of blessed foodstuffs is another loving reciprocation between the spiritual master and the disciple.

> The spiritual master's duty is to engage his disciples in preparing varieties of nice foods to offer to the Deity. After being offered, this food is distributed as *prasādam* to the devotees. These activities satisfy the spiritual master, although he himself does not eat or require such a variety of *prasādam*. By seeing the offering and distribution of *prasādam,* he himself is encouraged in devotional service.
>
> —Cc. *Madhya* 14.36

I personally feel I was saved by Śrīla Prabhupāda's liberal distribution of *prasādam,* just as a wretched, homeless dog is saved by the charity of a kind person who feeds him. I have recorded this in my memoirs of Śrīla Prabhupāda's Sunday feasts at 26 Second Ave. in New York, 1966:

> Eating the feast was an intense experience. We were supposed to be subduing our senses all week, following strict regulations, controlling the tongue. And the feast was a kind of reward. Swamiji and Kṛṣṇa were giving us a taste of full spiritual ecstasy, even though we were still beginners and still in the material world. Before taking my plateful, I would pray, "Please let me remain in Kṛṣṇa consciousness, because it is so nice and I am so fallen. Let me serve Swamiji, and let me enjoy this feast in transcendental bliss."
>
> —*Planting the Seed,* pg. 245

Once, when Śrīla Prabhupāda heard that devotees at a temple were not taking *prasādam* due to inconvenience and due to preference for other "healthier" diets, he became disturbed. "Why should we not be liking to take *kṛṣṇa-prasāda* in the temple?" he asked. "What is the fault? Everyone should take *prasādam*. It is called *prasāda-sevā,* service, not *prasāda*-enjoyment. *Prasādam* is as good as Kṛṣṇa and should be respected as much as Kṛṣṇa."

From these evidences we can see how the spiritual master becomes pleased when his disciples take *bhāgavata-prasāda*. Because he has great faith that *prasādam* is not material, the spiritual master is confident that when his disciples honor *prasādam,* their going back to Godhead is assured. Thus both he and his disciples become happy and successful simply by sharing the palatable *mahā-prasādam*. The *guru* introduces us to this merciful form of Kṛṣṇa as *prasādam*. And he teaches us that while taking *prasādam* we should call upon Lord Caitanya and Lord Nityānanda to please help us in devotional service.

5

The spiritual master is always eager to hear and chant about the unlimited conjugal pastimes of Rādhikā and Mādhava and Their qualities, names, and forms. The spiritual master aspires to relish these at every moment. I offer my respectful obeisances unto the lotus feet of such a spiritual master.

6

The spiritual master is very dear, because he is expert in assisting the *gopīs*, who at different times make different tasteful arrangements for the perfection of Rādhā and Kṛṣṇa's conjugal loving affairs within the groves of Vṛndāvana. I offer my most humble obeisances unto the lotus feet of such a spiritual master.

Inevitably, esoteric questions come to the mind of the disciple regarding the *guru's* eternal *rasa* with Kṛṣṇa and whether the disciple has a relationship with Kṛṣṇa in that same *rasa*. In 1968, Upendra dāsa asked Śrīla Prabhupāda: "When one has become pure enough, does one take regular dictation from his Guru Mahārāja? How is this so? Understanding that each individual has a certain particular rasa with Kṛṣṇa, how would one relate with another soul of a different rasa? Especially between that of the *guru* and disciple?" Śrīla Prabhupāda's reply to this neophyte question indicated that the guru is always expert to lead his disciple to the higher stages—and Śrīla Prabhupāda also offered caution.

The Spiritual Master's position is to train the disciples. Just like a teacher, he may be a very expert mathematician, but in the lower class he is teaching English. The Spiritual Master's duty is to train him, but when he comes to the perfectional stage of training, then he realizes his position. That is not a gift of the Spiritual Master, the Spiritual Master helps him to realize his relationship with the Lord. Just like the student in lower stages has to study so many things as preliminary education, English, history, math, etc., but in higher stage of education, he has got a particular taste for a special subject, so he specializes as a mathematician or a historian, etc. So that special qualification reveals in the higher stage. So these topics are not to be discussed in the conditioned stage, and when we come to the liberated stage we can understand. This is useless talks in the preliminary stage. In the beginning let us do the preliminary routine work very nicely, and be cured of the disease (out of maya), then we can know what taste you have for what particular type of food. So these things are not to be discussed at the present moment.

—Letter, November 13, 1968 to Upendra dāsa

The Vaiṣṇava *guru* is regularly serving Rādhā and Kṛṣṇa. He arranges for Their swing for Jhulana-yātrā, and he helps to decorate Śrīmatī Rādhārāṇī, Lalitā, and Viśākā in the groves of Vṛndāvana. He directly takes part in such pastimes and encourages his disciples to join him. In another way—as a preacher, arranging for *saṅkīrtana*—the spiritual master is attempting to bring the fallen souls back into their constitutional position, and he urges them to enter their relationship with the devotees of Rādhā and Kṛṣṇa in Vṛndāvana. This is especially accomplished when the spiritual master engages devotees in chanting the Hare Kṛṣṇa *mantra*: "Oh, Rādhārāṇī! Oh, Kṛṣṇa! Please engage me in Your service." When disciples assist the spiritual master in these activities, they are also acting as assistants of the *gopis*. The spiritual master has the responsibility of directly assisting the intimate servants of the Lord, and the disciples participate, under his direction, as his servants.

This spirit of assisting in the devotional mood of the spiritual master was displayed in its highest form when Svarūpa Dāmodara and Rāmānanda Rāya assisted Lord Caitanya in His mood of seperation from Kṛṣṇa . Svarūpa Dāmodara would sing songs exactly suitable for Śrī Caitanya Mahāprabhu's transcendental emotions, and Rāmānanda Rāya would quote verses from the writings of Vidyāpati, Cāṇḍidāsa, and Jayadeva Gosvāmī to compliment the ecstacy of Śrī Caitanya Mahāprabhu. Lord Caitanya would pass half the night experiencing varieties of emotions, and finaly Svarūpa Dāmodara and Rāmānanda Rāya, after making the Lord lie down on His bed, would return to their homes. Then Śrī Caitanya Mahāprabhu's personal servant, Govinda, would lie down at the door while the Lord loudly chanted the Hare Kṛṣṇa *mantra* all night.

Although this level of reciprocation cannot be duplicated or imitated, the disciple should appreciate that he is factually serving Rādhā and Kṛṣṇa as his spiritual master's instrument. The disciple is confident that by cleaning the temple floor as his spiritual master has asked him to he is also cleaning his heart through a direct relationship with Rādhā and Kṛṣṇa. The disciple cannot presume, however, to fully understand the mind of the spiritual master! *Vaiṣṇavera kriyā-mudrā vijñeha nā bujhaya.*

Once several disciples asked Śrīla Prabhupāda if their relationship with him could advance through the stages of servitude, friendship, parental, and conjugal. Prabhupāda said no, this was an improper understanding. The real relationship, he said, was expressed in the song *Śrī Guru-vandanā: janme janme prabhu sei.* "He is my lord, birth after birth." On another occasion, when disciples asked if Śrīla Prabhupāda was the eternal father of his disciples, he smiled and said, "I think so." And again he quoted the verse from *Śrī Guru-vandanā,* this time changing the word *prabhu* (master) to *pitā* (father)—*janme janme pitā sei.*

As Śrīla Prabhupāda indicated in his letter to Upendra dāsa, the higher realizations about a devotee's eternal relationships with Kṛṣṇa in the spiritual world will be fully revealed in the course of time, and one should wait patiently while laboriously serving the *guru* in many different ways. Certainly the spiritual master is assisting Rādhā and Kṛṣṇa, and certainly his sincere disciples are assisting him; but too many questions about the particular *rasas* will only serve as mental distractions and will not be beneficial or even comprehensible. The disciples prime work is to assist the spiritual master in rescuing the fallen souls, who in most cases have not the slightest spiritual understanding. By directly assisting the spiritual master in preaching, the disciple will become eligible to understand more and more about Kṛṣṇa.

7

The spiritual master is to be honored as much as the Supreme Lord because he is the most confidential servitor of the Lord. This is acknowledged in all revealed scriptures and followed by all authorities. Therefore I offer my respectful obeisances unto the lotus feet of such a spiritual master, who is a bona fide respresentative of Śrī Hari, [Kṛṣṇa].

The *śāstra* and the *sādhu* affirm that the spiritual master should be honored as much as God, and therefore we accept. If we accept that God should be honored as God, the greatest, then we should have no difficulty accepting His "viceroy." Nor is it wrong for the viceroy to present his own credentials. As long as he is genuine, the citizens must accept his words as coming directly from the king. Similarly, the spiritual master should be accepted on the strength of his symptoms and credentials. He must be in disciplic line from a bona fide spiritual master, and he must act and speak always as the representative of Kṛṣṇa. To such a genuine representative of Lord Kṛṣṇa we should offer our obeisances.

> Anyone, therefore, who takes shelter of the lotus feet of a pure devotee by accepting the pure devotee as his spiritual master can be at once purified. Such devotees of the Lord are honored equally with the Lord because they are engaged in the most confidential service of the Lord, for they deliver out of the material world the fallen souls whom the Lord wants to return home, back to Godhead. Such pure devotees are better known as vicelords according to revealed scriptures. The sincere disciple of the pure devotee considers the spiritual master equal to the Lord, but always considers himself to be a humble servant of the servant of the Lord. This is the pure devotional path.
>
> —*Bhāg*. 1.1.15

We have already described how the misbehavior of persons claiming to be *sādhus* and *gurus* is the greatest disservice to human society. Now because of such fraudulent spiritualists, someone may claim that he can no longer trust in *any* spiritual master. There is a Bengali proverb, however, that cautions against becoming foolishly angry and disappointed. We should not be like the man who ate his meals on the floor just because someone stole his plates. The sane logic is that is one's plates are stolen by a thief, one should not become angry and decide never again to purchase new plates. If a disappointed spiritual aspirant decides that finding an honest, authorized spiritual master is hopeless, then he cheats himself. It is true that in Kali-yuga the light of knowledge is covered by clouds of fraudulent practice, but it is also true that genuine representatives of the light of the *Bhāgavatam* are streaming forth as the sincere and ardent followers of Śrīla Prabhupāda. When we hear about and see for ourselves the genuine symptoms and credentials of a real spiritual master, we should gladly accept him and honor him as the most respectable personality. And we should appreciate his transcendental identity. This view is upheld "in all revealed scriptures and followed by all authorities."

8

> By the mercy of the spiritual master one receives the benediction of Kṛṣṇa. Without the grace of the spiritual master, one cannot make any advancement. Therefore, I should always remember and praise the spiritual master. At least three times a day I should offer my respectful obeisances unto the lotus feet of my spiritual master.

At least three times a day the formal prayers should be offered, but the remembrance and praise of the spiritual master should be continual. Especially after receiving his orders, the disciple should think about these orders constantly and not be disturbed by anything else. According to Viśvanātha Cakravartī Ṭhākura, the order of the spiritual master is the life and soul of the disciple. Meditation on his order is the perfection of meditation, and sincere attempts to carry out that order are the perfection of human activity.

When the spiritual master is pleased, then the disciple's highest objectives are achieved and he becomes more encouraged to go on carrying out the order of the spiritual master. He wants to please his spiritual master more and more, and there is no limit in the exchange. By this reciprocal energy the preaching of Kṛṣṇa consciousness goes on. A disciple's satisfaction, to please the previous spiritual masters in disciplic succession, is secured when he faithfully practices and preaches. To the degree a disciple carries out the spiritual master's order he can satisfy *guru* and Kṛṣṇa and subsequently satisfy himself.

As recorded in the *Caitanya-caritāmṛta*, Īśvara Purī, the spiritual master of Śrī Caitanya Mahāprabhu, performed service to Mādhavendra Purī in the last, difficult days of his spiritual master's life on earth. Īśvara Purī intimately cared for the body of his spiritual master and was always chanting the holy name and pastimes of Lord Kṛṣṇa for Mādhavendra Purī to hear. In this way, he helped Mādhavendra Purī remember the holy name and pastimes of Lord Kṛṣṇa at the time of death. Mādhavendra Purī was very pleased and gave Īśvara Purī the benediction that he would become a great devotee and lover of Kṛṣṇa. Kṛṣṇadāsa Kavirāja remarks that for this reason Īśvara Purī became an ocean of ecstatic love of Kṛṣṇa, whereas Rāmacandra Purī—who offended his spiritual master—became a dry speculator and critic of everyone else. "These two persons, Īśvara Purī and Rāmacandra Purī," writes Kṛṣṇadāsa Kavirāja, "are examples of the object of a great personality's benediction and punishment. Mādhavendra Purī instructed the entire world by presenting these two examples." (Cc. *Antya* 8.32)

If the spiritual master is displeased with a disciple, then that disciple's progress is blocked. Since the *guru* is even more concerned for his disciple that the wayward disciple for himself, the *guru* continues to instruct him, in hopes that he will rectify and take up his constitutional service before it's too late. When a wife came and forcibly dragged away one of Bhaktisiddhānta Sarasvatī's *sannyāsī* disciples, Bhaktisiddhānta Sarasvatī cried, "I could not save the soul."

His Divine Grace Śrīla Prabhupāda compassionately granted Vaiṣṇava initiation to thousands of men and women, and he always tried to save them from *guru-aparādha* (offenses to the *guru*), even when he saw them drifting away.

> Know it that I am eternally your guide, but if you don't accept me as your guide what can I do? Unfortunately, if my disciples do not take my guidance what can I do? By bad association it so happens, so I remain silent. I see the pricks of maya.
>
> You mentioned that your pathway has become filled with stumbling blocks, but there are not stumbling blocks, I can kick out all those stumbling blocks immediately, provided you accept my guidance. With one stroke of my kick, I can kick out all stumbling blocks.
>
> —Letter, September 9. 1972 to Kṛṣṇa dāsa

The secret of success in devotional service is to follow the order of the *guru*. Otherwise, a devotee becomes *āsāra,* or useless. One should mold his life so that all his thoughts and actions are directed toward carrying out the orders of his spiritual master. In this way, one realizes directly his eternal relationship with Kṛṣṇa. This is the essence of Vaiṣṇava behavior.

Chanting His Holy Name

The spiritual master introduces us to devotional service to Kṛṣṇa by engaging us in hearing and chanting the holy name. By hearing and chanting we come to understand that the holy name is Kṛṣṇa Himself. By hearing and chanting we can directly associate with the Supreme Lord, remove all dirty things from our hearts, and attain pure love of Kṛṣṇa.

First we have to hear from the *guru* and *śāstra* about the absolute nature of the holy name of Kṛṣṇa.

pūrṇaḥ śuddho nitya-mukto
'bhinnatvān nāma-nāminoḥ

> Kṛṣṇa's name is always liberated and spiritual; it is never conditioned by the laws of material nature. This is because the name of Kṛṣṇa and Kṛṣṇa Himself are identical.
>
> —*Padma Pūrana*

nāmnām akāri bahudhā nija-sarva-śaktis
tatrārpitā niyamitaḥ smaraṇe na kālaḥ

> In these transcendental names You have invested all Your transcendental energies.
>
> —*Śikṣāṣṭaka* #2

When we accept, at least theoretically, that the holy name is Kṛṣṇa, the Supreme Personality of Godhead, then we can begin chanting effectively. The absolute benefit is present, even if we chant the name negligently. The *śāstra* states, "If one, even accidentally, touches a spark of fire, the spark will burn him. In the same way, the holy name of Kṛṣṇa burns away all the sins of the chanter." Also, in the *Śrī-kṛṣṇa-nāmāṣṭakam* (verse #2) Śrīla Rūpa Gosvāmī writes, "Even if You (the holy name of Kṛṣṇa) are spoken carelessly or contemptuously, You at once remove all the harsh sufferings of the living entities."

The recommended cure for inattentive or offensive chanting is to go on constantly chanting and try to improve. As it is with our relationship with the spiritual master, so it is with our relationship with the holy name. We have to cultivate the relationship by avoiding offenses before we can get the desired result, love of Kṛṣṇa. Offenses to the holy name are known as *nāma-aparādha,* and they must be removed at all costs. Other sins and offenses are washed away by the chanting of the holy name, but if one offends the holy name, there is no recourse. A devotee has to go on chanting and gradually rectify the poor quality of his relationship with the holy name.

Lord Caitanya, praying in great humility said that because of offenses He could not taste the holy name as being Kṛṣṇa Himself, the reservoir of all beauty, opulence, strength, wisdom, fame, and renunciation. Rūpa Gosvāmī made a similar statement in the *Upadeśāmṛta,* where he compared material life to the disease of jaundice, which makes its victims unable to taste sugar as sweet. The man conditioned by material desires is unable to taste the wonderful sweetness of the holy name of Kṛṣṇa. Kṛṣṇa is present on his tongue, but he cannot fully taste Him, due to offenses. Yet, by hearing the glories of the holy name and by chanting regularly, one will develop love of Kṛṣṇa through this most easily available form of devotional service.

Oh, Hari-nāma! You have manifested in two forms. One is the blissful form of the Supreme Personality of

> Godhead and the other is the sound vibration of His holy name. We know that Your form as the sound vibration of the holy name is more merciful than that of Your blissful form. Even if one has committed the multitude of offenses to Your first form, by serving the second form with his voice he becomes always immersed in the ocean of transcendental bliss.
>
> —*Śrī-kṛṣṇa-nāmāṣṭakam* #6

Another principle that is very important in developing our relationship with the *guru* and also with the holy name is obedience. Although one may be struggling with inattentive, tasteless chanting, if he goes on serving the holy name obediently, then Kṛṣṇa will be pleased to reveal Himself. Rūpa Gosvāmī expresses this hope in *Nāmāṣṭakam* as follows: "If you wish, please appear constantly upon my tongue along with transcendental affection for the Lord."

Our relationship with the holy name is not something we can force. It is not mechanical, but depends upon the quality of our chanting. Kṛṣṇa will be especially pleased to reveal Himself when our chanting reaches the stage of genuine helplessness and we begin to cry out to the Lord. Kṛṣṇadāsa Kavirāja, the author of *Śrī Caitanya-caritāmṛta,* advises everyone to string the verse of the *Śikṣāṣṭaka** on the thread of the holy name "and wear it around your neck for continuous remembrance." This verse tells how we should chant the Hare Kṛṣṇa *mantra* to very easily awaken our dormant love for Kṛṣṇa.

In the beginning one will commit offenses in chanting, and at that stage there will be no possibility of achieving love of Kṛṣṇa. But if one chants regularly,

---

**Tṛṇād api sunīcena,* "One should chant the holy name of the Lord in a humble state of mind."

never abandoning his vow of obedience, and if he can enter the humble, forbearing spirit of the *Śikṣāṣṭaka* verse, then he can learn to chant Hare Kṛṣṇa constantly and humbly and thereby please the Lord. "Chanting is very simple," comments Śrīla Prabhupāda, "but one must practice it seriously." All the eternal associates of Lord Caitanya took part in chanting the Hare Kṛṣṇa *mantra* as their life-sustaining activity. And any devotee today who aspires to follow the *mahājanas* must first and foremost be a chanter of the holy name.

Worshipping the Deity

The *madhyama-bhakta's* relationship with Kṛṣṇa starts by chanting and hearing the holy name and by hearing the scriptures. The *Bhagavad-gītā* is Śrī Kṛṣṇa's own words, and *Śrīmad-Bhāgavatam* is described as "a literary incarnation of God." Hearing and speaking the verses of such scriptures is the same as the *kīrtana* of the Hare Kṛṣṇa *mantra*. If the topic is Kṛṣṇa, the Supreme Personality of Godhead, and if the speaker is authorized, then any form of glorifications is absolute. Prahlāda Mahārāja recommended nine methods of devotional service, beginning with hearing, chanting, and remembering Lord Viṣṇu, and including serving the Lord's lotus feet and worshiping the Deity.

Because Kṛṣṇa is a person and because devotional service is exchanged between persons (the devotee and the Lord), the worship of the Lord's personal form as the Deity is particularly important. In the *Bhagavad-gītā* Kṛṣṇa declares that worshiping Him and His personal form is better than meditating on the formless, impersonal *brahman*, and He specifically requests that a worshiper make devotional offerings of water, fruit, and vegetables. But since thousands of years have passed since Lord Kṛṣṇa spoke the *Bhagavad-gītā* and appeared on the earth in His original form, we may ask how we can render such intimate service to His personal form today? The answer is that Kṛṣṇa mercifully consents to appear in His *arcā-vigraha* (Deity form) just to facilitate the devotional service of a devotee who cannot yet see the all-spiritual form of the Personality of Godhead.

Because the devotees in the material world can see only the material elements, Kṛṣṇa kindly appears in wood or stone or metal, and when these elements are wrought in the shape of Lord Kṛṣṇa as is described in the scriptures, then that Deity form is nondifferent from Lord Kṛṣṇa. The atheist cannot believe that God can appear in the form of a statue, but neither can he give a convincing reason why He should be unable to do so if He pleases. The *śāstras* warn, *arcye viṣṇau śilā dhīḥ*: "One should never think of the *arcā-mūrti*, the Deity within the temple, as stone, wood, or any other material element." The Deity can act exactly as the Lord does in His original form of Kṛṣṇa. Devotees who understand the science of Kṛṣṇa and who behold Him with eyes of love can directly talk with the Deity, and Kṛṣṇa has no difficulty in replying to their prayers or receiving their offerings.

In His incarnation as Lord Kapila, Lord Kṛṣṇa explained to Devahūti how the pure devotees are pleased to see His personal form, whether in the spiritual world or in the *arcā-vigraha* within the temple.

> O, My mother, My devotees always see the smiling face of My form, with eyes like the rising morning sun. They like to see My various transcendental forms, which are all benevolent, and they also talk favorably with Me.
>
> —*Bhāg*. 3.25.35

A doubt may be raised whether it is absolutely necessary to worship the Deity. Since the holy name of Kṛṣṇa, the Hare Kṛṣṇa *mantra,* contains the full presence of Lord Kṛṣṇa, why does a devotee have to undergo the brahminical initiation and particular activities of Deity service? Isn't the chanting enough?

The answer is that chanting is certainly enough, but constant chanting is especially for the liberated soul. Śrīla Prabhupāda writes, "Even though the chanting of the holy name is sufficient to enable one to progress in spiritual life to the standard of love of Godhead, one is nonetheless susceptible to contamination because of possessing a material body. Consequently, a special stress is given to the *arcana-vidhi.* One should therefore regularly take advantage of both the *bhāgavata* process and the *pāncarātrikī* process." (*Bhāg.* 7.5.24, purport) For the conditioned souls of Kali-yuga, Śrīla Jīva Gosvāmī recommends that Deity worship in the temple be compulsory. Nor did any of the liberated *ācāryas* ever discourage temple worship; rather, they set the example for the masses of people by arranging for the construction of grand temples and installing Deities of Rādhā-Kṛṣṇa or Lakṣmī-Nārāyaṇa. When Nārada Muni instructed the young Dhruva Mahārāja to perform *mantra* meditation in the jungle, he also advised that Dhruva make a simple Deity form and perform *arcā-sevā.*

In His Deity form, Kṛṣṇa becomes malleable and dependent on His devotee's care. The worship must, therefore, be rendered with enthusiasm and precise attention. The devotee must sew opulent clothes for the Deity, artistically decorate the Deity, clean the temple, perform many *āratis* daily, cook the best foods available to offer the Deity, and carry out all the routine activities of Deity worship without fail. Through this meditation and service, the *pūjārī* gives up his material desires and enters into a very personal relationship with the Lord. Sometimes he dreams of the Deity, and the Deity makes particular requests. "Even in the form of stone or metal," says Śrīla Prabhupāda in *Teachings of Queen Kunti,* "Kṛṣṇa can act as Kṛṣṇa, and one who worships the Deity will perceive that. *Svayam eva sphuraty adaḥ.* The Deity, although apparently stone, may speak with a devotee." At the time of death, if the Deity worshiper remembers and sees before him the personal form of Lord Kṛṣṇa, he will immediately attain to eternal devotional service in the spiritual world.

Whether one approaches Kṛṣṇa through chanting, worshiping the Deity, or hearing the scriptures—all, of course, under the guidance of Kṛṣṇa's representative, the spiritual master—the characteristics of a personal relationship with Kṛṣṇa will develop. For example, a devotee will come to depend on Kṛṣṇa. Whether he is alone or with others, a steadfast devotee knows he is never alone: Kṛṣṇa is in his heart. "To those who are constantly devoted to serving Me with love," Lord Kṛṣṇa states, "I give the understanding by which they can come to Me." (Bg. 10.10)

Also, a devotee comes to consider himself Kṛṣṇa's property. He does only what is favorable to Kṛṣṇa's devotional service, and he avoids whatever is unfavorable. Lord Kṛṣṇa assures His surrendered devotees that He will always protect them and that His relationship with them is His main concern. "My devotees do not know anything else but Me," Lord Kṛṣṇa said to Durvāsa Muni, "and I do not know anyone else but them." (*Bhāg.* 9.4.68) Although Lord Kṛṣṇa is described as *ātmārāma,* self-satisfied, He is particularly inclined with affection to those who are surrendered at His lotus feet.

Having attained an intimate service relationship with Kṛṣṇa, a devotee doesn't desire anything within the material world, not is he interested in liberation. Kṛṣṇa is always inclined toward his pure devotees, but the pure devotee never asks Him for any help or reward. If he does ask for anything, it is that he never be deviated in the course of his devotional service. Sometimes Kṛṣṇa tests His devotee, and when His devotee is successful, the importance of his relationship with Kṛṣṇa is magnified and the bond between them becomes purer and tighter.

As part of his exclusive attachment to Kṛṣṇa, the pure devotee sees Kṛṣṇa in all living entities. Realizing that everyone is related to Kṛṣṇa, he works to help revive the original Kṛṣṇa consciousness in the hearts of those who are covered with forgetfulness. In this way, love of Kṛṣṇa radiates to all living beings in the universe and the devotee becomes everyone's well-wisher. By offering his love to Kṛṣṇa and always glorifying Him, the *madhyama-bhakta* benefits whomever he meets. A pure devotee's relationship with Kṛṣṇa is ever fresh and infinite, as Kṛṣṇa Himself, and it cannot be fully described, not even by Anantadeva.

THE MADHYAMA-BHAKTA IS

A Sincere Friend to all the Devotees of the Lord

We have just discussed how the *madhyama-bhakta* offers his love to the Supreme Personality of Godhead through the spiritual master, the holy name, and the Deity of Kṛṣṇa. Now we shall consider the Vaiṣṇava behavior of the *madhyama-bhakta* as expressed in his relationships with other devotees.

The devotees of Kṛṣṇa are friends. "The thoughts of My pure devotees dwell in Me," says Lord Kṛṣṇa, "their lives are fully devoted to My service, and they derive great satisfaction and bliss from always enlightening one another and conversing about Me." (Bg. 10.9) The *śāstras* strongly advise associating with like-minded devotees, and strongly warn against association with nondevotees. The *śāstras* also contain many instructions about various kinds of relationship between the various kinds of devotees, and these teachings form an important part of Vaiṣṇava etiquette.

In one sense, all devotees may be considered as a single class, as sincere followers of Lord Kṛṣṇa. Śrīla Prabhupāda writes in a *Caitanya-caritāmṛta* purport, "Śrīla Kṛṣṇadāsa Kavirāja sets the example of offering obeisances to all the preacher devotees of Lord Caitanya, without distinction as to higher and lower."

> I offer my obeisances to all the dear devotees of Śrī Caitanya Mahāprabhu, the eternal tree of love of Godhead. I offer my respects to all the branches of the tree, the devotees of the Lord who distribute the fruit of love of Kṛṣṇa.
>
> —Cc. *Ādi* 10.7

The devotees are all personalists who glorify the Supreme Person with transcendental chanting and hearing, and they take pleasure in the company of other personal servitors of the Lord. "A pure devotee does not desire the company of a personality as great as Brahmā," writes Śrīla Prabhupāda, "but he prefers the association of a petty living being provided he is a devotee of the Lord." (*Bhāg*. 1.19.16, purport)

One time while Lord Caitanya was viewing the Deity of Lord Jagannātha from the rear of the temple at Jagannātha Purī, an Orissan woman suddenly climbed the column of Garuḍa and placed her foot on Śrī

Caitanya Mahāprabhu's shoulder. When the devotees of Lord Caitanya saw this they were aghast, and Lord Caitanya's personal servant, Govinda, got the woman down. Lord Caitanya, however, chastised Govinda and said, "O *ādi-vasyā* [uncivilized man], do not forbid this woman to climb the Garuḍa-stambha. Let her see Lord Jagannātha to her satisfaction." (Cc. *Antya* 14.26) Not only did Lord Caitanya excuse the woman's grievous offenses of stepping of Garuḍa and Himself, but He even praised her eagerness and said, "Lord Jagannātha has not bestowed so much eagerness upon Me." By this example He showed that even the most exalted personality may consider himself edified by the sincere devotion of the lowest of Vaiṣṇavas.

Once a great devotee, Puṇḍarīka Vidyānidhi, was punished by Lord Jagannātha Himself, when Puṇḍarīka Vidyānidhi felt some hatred for a simple *pūjārī* who committed a slight discrepancy in dressing Lord Jagannātha. Lord Jagannātha and Lord Balarāma both appeared to Puṇḍarīka Vidyānidhi in a dream and, smiling, began to slap him until his cheeks were swollen, warning him not to be offensive to any Vaiṣṇava.

When a devotee wrote to Śrīla Prabhupāda, praising his own Godbrothers, Śrīla Prabhupāda replied:

> This is actually a devotee's business that everyone should appreciate the value of other devotees. Nobody should criticize anyone. Because everyone is engaged in the service of the Lord, according to one's capacity, and the thing is, Krishna wants to see how much one is sincere in rendering Him service. Materially we may think that his service is greater than his, that is our material vision. Actually on the spiritual platform, the service rendered by a calf to Krishna and service rendered by Radharani and Her Associates, to Krishna,

there is no difference. Krishna is so kind and liberal that everyone's service, when it is sincerely offered to Krishna, He accepts.

—Letter, August 19, 1968, to Tamāla Kṛṣṇa dāsa

Nevertheless, the Vaiṣṇava scholars have analyzed that there are different categories of devotees and different attitudes of general behavior to be followed in devotional interactions.

"One should mentally honor any devotee who chants the holy name of Lord Kṛṣṇa," states Rūpa Gosvāmī. (Upadeśāmṛta #5) Thus Rūpa Gosvāmī describes in brief the *kaniṣṭha-adhikārī,* or beginning devotee. The *kaniṣṭha-adhikārī* has the disqualifications of not properly respecting advanced devotees and not perceiving Lord Kṛṣṇa within the hearts of all living beings. Mostly he recognizes Kṛṣṇa's presence only in the Deity within the temple. Yet even the *kaniṣṭha-adhikārī* is far greater than all the nondevotees who are classified as either *karmīs* (gross materialists) or *yogīs* and *jñānīs* (impersonal transcendentalists). Because he is a devotee of the Supreme Personality of Godhead, the *kaniṣṭha-adhikārī* is a first-class transcendentalist, he is rare and wonderful in this world. *A kaniṣṭha-adhikārī* is sometimes also called a materialistic devotee, because he has a tendency to be interested in material benefits. Therefore a devotee must strive to make progress to come to the second-class position, the *madhyama-bhakta.*

"The *madhyama-adhikārī,"* writes Śrīla Prabhupāda, "has received spiritual initiation from the spiritual master and has been fully engaged by him in the transcendental loving service of the Lord."

Śrīla Prabhupāda also describes the highest stage or *uttama-adhikārī*:

> Out of many such Vaiṣṇavas, one may be found to be very seriously engaged in the service of the Lord and strictly following all the regulative principles, chanting the prescribed number of rounds on *japa* beads, and always thinking of how to expand the Kṛṣṇa consciousness movement. Such a Vaiṣṇava should be accepted as an *uttama-adhikārī,* a highly advanced devotee, and his association should always be sought.
>
> —*Upadeśāmṛta* #5, purport

Rūpa Gosvāmī explains that one should mentally honor the beginner, or materialistic devotee, one should offer humble obeisances to the *madhyama* devotee, and associate with and faithfully serve the pure devotee, "who is advanced in undeviated devotional service and whose heart is completely devoid of the propensity to criticize others." (*Upadeśamṛta* #5)

Although all devotees should receive our honor, there are clear guidelines for dealing with the different classes of devotees. Every devotee will find himself in a situation where some devotees are more advanced than he, some are his peers, and some are newcomers or less advanced. According to Vaiṣṇava behavior, one should inquire from and render service to the more advanced devotees, one should make loving friendships with equal devotees, and one should give merciful guidance to those who are more neophyte than oneself.

Serving More Advanced Devotees

The disciple accepts the spiritual master to be as good as God. Of course, the spiritual master never claims to be God, and if he did, he would be completely disqualified. An individual spiritual soul can never be equal in all respects to God, but the spiritual master is the confidential servitor of God. Among devotees, therefore, the spiritual master holds a unique position, but a devotee will honor other advanced Vaiṣṇavas *almost* one a level with his spiritual master. Śrīla Prabhupāda described how Lord Caitanya honored Advaitācārya as a "spiritual uncle," because he was a Godbrother of Lord Caitanya's *guru*, Īśvara Purī. "Thus Advaita Prabhu, as Lord Caitanya's spiritual uncle, was always to be respected," Śrīla Prabhupāda writes, "because one should respect one's spiritual master's Godbrothers as one respects one's spiritual master." (Cc. *Ādi* 5.147, purport)

Whenever a devotee gets an opportunity to hear from or serve an advanced Vaiṣṇava, he should remember the sastric injuctions and go forward with great eagerness to honor the devotee. If there is an imbalance between two disciples, a devotee should not be envious. Śrīla Prabhupāda writes, "If a Godbrother is more enlightened and advanced in Kṛṣṇa consciousness, one should accept him as almost equal to the spiritual master, and one should be happy to see such Godbrothers advance in Kṛṣṇa consciousness." (*Bhāg.* 3.32.42, purport) *Śrīmad-Bhāgavatam* also states, "The value of a moment's association with the devotees of the Lord cannot be even compared to the attainment of heavenly planets or liberation from matter, and what to speak of worldly benedictions in the form of material prosperity, which are for those who are meant for death." (*Bhāg.* 1.18.13)

But how, someone may well ask, do we know who is an advanced devotee? Is every Godbrother of the spiritual master really deserving to be accepted as almost equal to one's *guru*? Is every *sannyāsī* or senior devotee to be considered advanced?

If a senior devotee's or *sannyāsī's* behavior does not correspond with the symptoms for proper Vaiṣṇava behavior, then one has to judge for oneself; but even if one does not see symptoms of advancement, he should continue to observe the etiquette befitting senior devotees and *sannyāsīs.* This manner of behavior was demonstrated by Lord Caitanya who continued to honor a senior *sannyāsī,* Rāmācandra Purī, even though Rāmācandra Purī behaved offensively in many ways. When individual cases become extremely subtle, one should consult respectable devotees for guidance in how to behave.

An example of a most baffling case is that of Aśvattāmā who, although the son of a *brāhmaṇa,* was a great offender to the Lord and the Lord's devotees. He had murdered the five sleeping sons of Draupadī. When Arjuna captured him, Bhīma thought Aśvatthāmā should be killed, while Yudhiṣṭhira and Draupadī thought he should be spared. Arjuna, however, through careful consideration and with inspiration from Lord Kṛṣṇa, came up with a suitable solution. Thus we have this example that, despite the difficulties of making judgments, one should refer to the standard guides of Vaiṣṇava behavior. We must be guided by *guru, śāstra,* and *sādhu* and not sentimentally assess things only from our intuitive likes and dislikes.

The Vedic law books, however, have to be understood and applied according to time and place, and this must be done by the authorized devotee, for as we have already discussed, great authorities must set the example in what is to be done and what is not to be done in the course of devotional service. Citing a reference from a scripture and making a quick judgment will not always do, nor is lenience always justified. As Śrīla Bhagavān Goswami wrote in his Vyāsa-pūjā offering of 1983, "May we learn from you (Śrīla Prabhupāda) how to avoid blind justice or foolish mercy/ Both of which create havoc in the house."

Friendships with Equal Devotees

With whom are we equal in devotional service? A humble devotee tends to think he is less than others, and he will hesitate to consider with whom he is spiritually equal. Immature devotees, may make too much of social distinctions, as if a *gṛhastha* could never be spiritual equal to a *sannyāsī*, or as if a devotee of twelve years' standing could not be the equal of a devotee of sixteen years' standing. Yet "equals" really means equal-minded friends. Therefore, equals in devotional service form spiritual friendships.

Devotees with mutual or similar services on behalf of the spiritual master of devotees with similar natures and behavior tend to become friends in Kṛṣṇa consciousness. Without trying to pin down too many incidental criteria, however, let us simply say that some devotees are equals and form friendships. Of course no two individuals can be exactly equal in everything. Friendships are, therefore, give-and-take. A basis for the loving spiritual exchange between devotees is given by Rūpa Gosvāmī is *Upadeśāmṛta.*

> Offering gifts in charity, accepting charitable gifts, revealing one's mind in confidence, inquiring confidentially, accepting *prasāda,* and offering *prasāda* are the six symptoms of love shared by one devotee and another.
>
> —*Upadeśāmṛta* #4

Spiritual friendship is distinct from material friendship in that material friendship is based on sense gratification, whereas spiritual friendship is based on Kṛṣṇa consciousness. A person endeavoring for Kṛṣṇa consciousness should not seek out a friend for any material reason; a devotee has nothing to gain from a rich man or a political ally. Since we are no longer on the path of material progress, we should not be interested in bodily beauty, aristocratic birth, material wealth, or material education. All our friendships should intensify devotional service.

Sometimes, in mundane relationships, one "hangs out" with his friends as a kind of relief from the usual tension of one's business occupation. But a devotee is not looking for a companion with whom to engage in *prajalpa* (loose talk) or someone to gossip with or to engage with in subtle or gross forbidden acts. To have an enemy would be better than to have such a "friend" in the name of Kṛṣṇa consciousness. Kṛṣṇa conscious friendship, therefore, must always be within the bounds of Vaiṣṇava behavior and etiquette. Friends should conduct themselves so that they may impel each other's service attitude toward Kṛṣṇa and the spiritual master. In this way they relate according to the six loving exchanges described by Rūpa Gosvāmī.

Friends share the Lord's *prasādam* and exchange gifts that help one another in devotional service; and they share thoughts. Sometimes we need a friend of whom we can inquire confidentially. A devotee may be feeling weak-hearted, but he can express himself only to a trusted and confidential friend. His devotee-friend will then lovingly preach to him and try to remind him of the spiritual master's teachings, offering both sympathy and relevant instructions from the scriptures. Every devotee needs such close friends. The day will come when the one from whom I have inquired confidentially will return the confidential favor and approach me with some confidential sharing or inquiry of his own. Such confidential exchanges, however, should not become the basis of a clique or of clannish behavior. While we may select our intimate friends from the company of devotees, we should remain straightforward and ready to share our realizations with all sincere devotees.

Of course, Lord Caitanya selected a very few intimate devotees who assisted Him in His intimate feelings of separation from Kṛṣṇa. The *Caitanya-caritāmṛta* says that Rāmānanda Rāya and Svarūpa Dāmodara were able to stay always with Lord Caitanya's company even when He displayed the mood of Rādhārāṇi's madness in separation from Kṛṣṇa. In the spiritual world, certain devotees of the same *rasa* share eternal, intimate relations. Within the Kṛṣṇa consciousness movement, as devotees work side by side, they should make close friendships for improving their own spiritual lives and those of their devotional friends. The center should always be Kṛṣṇa. As we serve together of this basis, serving with our friends, chanting the holy name, and discussing the meaning of the *śāstras*, surely more and more will be revealed to us about the ultimate nature of friendships among devotees.

Giving Mercy to Less Advanced Devotees

The most obvious kind of less advanced devotee is the newcomer. He doesn't know the Vaiṣṇava philosophy well and is as yet uncertain in his commitment. Older devotees should help such a neophyte in any way possible. Persons who have spent years in the Kṛṣṇa consciousness movement but who have remained materially attached may also be less advanced devotees. Bhaktisiddhānta Sarasvatī was asked why devotees advanced at different rates. In reply he told the story of the wedding party. A group of people on their way to a wedding hired a boat for the river journey. The boatman rowed all night, but because he had forgotten to pull out the anchor, the boat never moved from the shore. Bhaktisiddhānta Sarasvatī drew the analogy: If a devotee does not pull up the anchor of material attachment and sense gratification, then despite all his show of devotional service, he will not advance.

Vaiṣṇavas, however, are merciful to less advanced devotees, especially when they detect a spark of sincerity and when they see that the less advanced devotee is at least convinced that Kṛṣṇa is the Supreme Personality of Godhead. Devotees are so kind that sometimes, even when a fallen devotee is rejected by the Supreme Lord, they still try to engage that devotee in devotional service so that he may become rectified. "The Lord Himself may sometimes be very hard," writes Śrīla Prabhupāda, "but the devotees are always kind. Thus Kāla Kṛṣṇadāsa received the mercy of Nityānanda Prabhu, Jagadānanda, Mukunda and Dāmodara." (Cc. *Madhya* 10.67, purport)

A Vaiṣṇava shows mercy by taking time to counsel and give relevant instructions and by making plans whereby the lesser devotees may engage in devotional service, thereby tasting the nectar of Kṛṣṇa consciousness.

But one cannot give anyone else mercy unless he himself is strictly following Vaiṣṇava behavior. The *Śrīmad-Bhāgavatam* describes that Lord Brahmā, the forefather of all living entities "situated himself in acts of regulative principles, desiring self interest for the welfare of all living entities." (*Bhāg*. 2.9.40) Śrīla Prabhupāda comments, "Pure devotees of the Lord, like Brahmā and persons in the chain of disciplic succession, do not do anything to instruct their subordinates without acting accordingly themselves."

In the name of supervising lesser devotees, a leader should never abuse them. When Śrīla Prabhupāda heard that a woman was engaging a Godsister as her personal servant, he corrected this mistaken etiquette. "Why Taittiriya should have a servant?" wrote Śrīla Prabhupāda. "Godbrothers are not meant for being servants. Without the spiritual master's order, nobody can utilize the service of a godbrother as one's personal servant. We address each other as prabhu, so how can we engage our godbrother as servant?" (Letter, November 11, 1974 to Kirtanānanda Swami)

On one occasion, when two Godbrothers were quarrelling as to who was in the superior position, Prabhupāda gave instructions to the devotee whom he recognized as the leader.

> As a matter of fact, as you are the pioneer in taking all risks to go to Australia, naturally you shall be considered as the leader, but a leader's position is also very grave and responsible. A leader has to leader others tactfully and intelligently. Kindly therefore do not quarrel, but go on with your duties progressively.
>
> —Letter, May 10, 1970 to Bali-mardana dāsa

Showing mercy to others is sometimes not an easy thing. If we give a thief the mercy of good moral instructions, he may become angry with us. And one must be competent to "tactfully and intelligently" extend mercy to lesser devotees. Giving mercy cannot be someone's concoction and cannot be done with a motivation to become praised and worshiped by lesser devotees. A devotee should remain humble and fixed in Kṛṣṇa conscious principles, and then he will be competent to give the mercy of his good example to others. If one behaves ideally, he will give mercy to everyone, without any extraneous effort.

In summary, a devotee will find himself obliged sometimes to give and sometimes to receive in his exchanges with the three classes of devotees. In doing so he should be guided by the principles of honor, friendship, and mercy.

> The pure devotee should execute devotional service by giving the greatest respect to the spiritual master and the *ācāryas*. He should be compassionate to the poor and make friendship with persons who are his equals, but all of his activities should be executed under regulation and with control of the senses.
>
> —*Bhāg*. 3.29.17

THE MADHYAMA-BHAKTA'S RELATIONSHIP TO THE INNOCENT NONDEVOTEES

A pure devotee has a naturally friendly disposition. He is not prone to cause anyone anxiety by words or even by ill thoughts. He forgives the wrongs of others. When this mood is combined with the understanding that the nondevotees are suffering and preparing themselves for more suffering, the devotee's compassion is activated, and he wants to render service to the fallen souls. All classes of men and women who are averse to hearing and chanting about Kṛṣṇa are pitiable because they are neglecting the real purpose of human life, and they will have to go on suffering repeated birth and death in the material world. They may be austere *yogīs* or learned scholars who do not accept the Supreme Personality of Godhead; they may be religionists who formally accept the existence of God but are after material gain; they may be various kinds of speculators, enjoyers, and agnostics. But all who avoid pure devotional service to the Supreme Personality of Godhead have an inauspicious existence. Only the devotees of

Lord Kṛṣṇa can see through the nondevotees' illusions and understand their plight; therefore, if the devotee doesn't come to their assistance, how can they be saved?

Out of compassion, the preacher approaches and tries to deliver all sinful persons. The devotee is not satisfied with his own salvation; he is anxious for the welfare of others. As he contacts the nondevotees, he finds some of them to be extremely inimical and blasphemous, whereas others he considers innocent. By innocent we do not mean that they are sinless, but that they are not directly blasphemous and, when confronted with Kṛṣṇa consciousness, are not inimical, although they may continue their abominable activities. If a devotee sees in a nondevotee the smallest spark of interest toward Kṛṣṇa, he works earnestly to fan that spark into a fire.

This attitude is inspired by Kṛṣṇa Himself, who, as the well-wishing Father of all living entities, wants everyone to give up their suffering and return to Him. The devotees, as faithful sons and daughters of the Supreme Father, work to bring about Lord Kṛṣṇa's desires for recovering His lost children. When the Lord sees His servants approaching others with His mercy, He is very satisfied. If a devotee fails to understand that all beings are related to Kṛṣṇa, and if he doesn't attempt to distribute Kṛṣṇa's mercy to them, he cannot make spiritual advancement just by executing prescribed duties.

Commenting upon Rūpa Gosvāmī's six exchanges of love among devotees, Śrīla Prabhupāda applies these exchanges to the relationship between preachers and the nondevotees, or near-devotees. Regarding the exchange of gifts, Prabhupāda says that he, as the founder-*ācārya* of ISKCON, is pleased to see that people are donating liberally to the Kṛṣṇa consciousness movement and that in return the devotees are offering them "a humble contribution" in the shape of Kṛṣṇa conscious books and magazines. The exchange of foodstuffs between devotees and innocent nondevotees has become world famous through ISKCON's worldwide distribution of *prasādam*. Regarding another symptom of such loving exchanges, Śrīla Prabhupāda writes, "Sometimes the members and supporters inquire very confidentially about the methods of performing devotional service, and we try to explain this" (*Upadeśāmṛta* #4, purport).

The pure devotee's dedication to the welfare work of helping the spiritually poor is so intense that he is willing to give up his life to bring it about. Prahlāda Mahārāja declared that he would forego his own return back to Godhead until all sinful persons could be saved and join with him at the lotus feet of Kṛṣṇa. Vāsudeva Datta, a *mahā-bhāgavata* devotee of Lord Caitanya, asked the Lord to please transfer all the karmic sufferings of all living beings in the universe to him, and to allow the sinners to return to the kingdom of God. And the saintly king, Mahārāja Rantideva, made a similar prayer.

> I do not pray to the Supreme Personality of Godhead for the eight perfections of mystic yoga, nor for salvation from repeated birth and death. I want only to stay among all the living entities and suffer all distresses on their behalf, so that they may be freed from suffering.
> —*Bhāg*. 9.21.12

These are examples of the perfection of Vaiṣṇava behavior. Lord Kṛṣṇa says that of all the servants of God, those who preach are the dearmost servants in the world to Him.

AVOIDING THE ASSOCIATION OF THE ATHEISTS

When Lord Caitanya was asked by a householder devotee what the behavior of a devotee should be, he immediately replied:

asat-saṅga-tyāga,—ei vaiṣṇava 'ācāra
strī-saṅgī'—eka asādhu, 'kṛṣṇābhakta' āra

> A Vaiṣṇava should always avoid the association of ordinary people. Common people are very much materially attached, especially to women. Vaiṣṇavas should also avoid the company of those who are not devotees of Lord Kṛṣṇa.
>
> —Cc. *Madhya* 22.87

It is, therefore, the very definition of a Vaiṣṇava that he avoid the association of persons inimical to devotional service. In citing factors unfavorable to devotional service, Rūpa Gosvāmī mentions, "associating with worldly-minded persons who are not interested in Kṛṣṇa consciousness." (*Upadeśamṛta* #2) *The Nectar of Devotion* gives the injunction with great force: "in the *Kātyāyana-saṁhitā* it is stated that even if one is forced to live within a cage of iron or in the midst of a blazing fire one should accept this position rather than live with nondevotees who are through and through against the supremacy of the Lord." (*Bhakti-rasāmṛta-sindhu* pg. 64)

Association is all-important. As the company of the *mahātmas* can open the door to liberation, so the company of degraded materialists can drag an aspiring devotee into ignorance. Persons fond of enjoying illicit sex and persons opposed to God consciousness destroy by their association the purity of Vaiṣṇava behavior. It is no wonder, therefore, that a devotee does not enjoy such association.

But is avoiding the association of nondevotees contradictory to the Lord's desire that sinful persons be delivered? According to Bhaktisiddhānta Sarasvatī Ṭhākura, as quoted by Hṛdayānanda Mahārāja in the Eleventh Canto of *Śrīmad-Bhāgavatam,* a devotee's avoiding atheists is quite in accord with the will of the Supreme Personality of Godhead. The *madhyama-bhakta* should avoid envious nondevotees so that he won't become disturbed or polluted by them. And he is also benefiting the envious by denying them the opportunity to commit further offenses against the Vaiṣṇavas. Hṛdayānanda Mahārāja explains this point in his purport.

> Śrīla Bhaktisiddhānta Sarasvatī Ṭhākura has given an elaborate explanation to prove that the discrimination employed by a *madhyama-adhikārī* preacher does not at all show a lack of mercy. He states that the *upekṣā,* or neglect, mentioned in the verse, is the proper medicine for those who are inimical to the Supreme Lord and His devotees. Indifference from the preacher checks feelings of hostility from both sides . . . It is the duty of a Vaiṣṇava preacher to point out the futility of any process besides surrendering to the Supreme Lord. An envious person, however, will resent such strong preaching by a Vaiṣṇava and disrespect him, considering the devotee to be unnecessarily criticizing others. Such a person, who cannot appreciate the mercy of the Vaiṣṇavas, should be neglected. Otherwise, according to Śrīla Bhaktisiddhānta Sarasvatī Ṭhākura his cheating mentality will increase day by day.
>
> —*Bhāg*. 11.2.46, purport

In describing the devotee's selective application of mercy toward the nondevotees, Śrīla Prabhupāda used what he called "the hospital rule." At a time of war or catastrophe, when the hospital is filled with more cases than can be treated, the doctors may neglect a patient in critical condition in favor of a patient who could be saved if given immediate attention. Similarly, the envious are too far gone, and when a devotee attempts to inform them of the glories of the Supreme Lord, their scornful response only worsens their condition. It is better for devotees to use their limited time and manpower in approaching innocent persons. This is sometimes referred to as "preaching where it is favorable." Lord Caitanya Himself abandoned extensive preaching in Navadvīpa, because the place was saturated with intellectual wranglers who refused to accept Lord Caitanya's teachings. He therefore preferred to travel through South India, where the people were more pious and receptive.

Yet despite the precautions against approaching atheists, preachers sometimes take the risk on behalf of Kṛṣṇa, and when they do so, Kṛṣṇa is pleased. It is difficult to find anyone nowadays who is not infected with demonic qualities. Devotees, therefore, sometimes come up against actively, envious demons, and avoiding them is not always possible. Lord Nityānanda and Haridāsa Ṭhākura managed to convert the drunkards, Jagāi and Mādhāi. But the general principle should be our guide: in considering the nondevotees, the preacher should approach those who are noninimical but should avoid the envious.

Basic Principles and Rules of Vaiṣṇava Behavior

HIS DIVINE GRACE Śrīla Prabhupāda stressed that all his followers must strictly follow the spiritual principles as an absolute requirement. He said he was trying to train first-class men—devotees of brahminical character who could, in turn, guide and uplift the lower divisions of society. The regulative principles are designed to take us gradually to the platform of spontaneous love of Kṛṣṇa, which is the perfection of human life. If a so-called devotee thinks he has already attained perfection and gives up the spiritual principles, then he is known as a *prākṛta-bhakta,* or one who takes things cheaply and merely imitates true devotional service.

Repeatedly, Śrīla Prabhupāda gave his students this overall direction: live with the devotees, rise early and attend *maṅgala-ārati,* chant 16 rounds of the *mahā-mantra* on beads, attend the *Śrīmad-Bhāgavatam* class, and read his books. And after attending a full morning's spiritual program, everyone should work all day in some honest service for Kṛṣṇa, under the order of the spiritual master. And the basic restrictions of avoiding the four pillars of sinful life—illicit sex, meat-eating, intoxications, and gambling—these things a devotee must avoid without fail, or there is no question of spiritual life.

Without following the spiritual principles, a devotee's enthusiasm dwindles, and degradation follows. These are the simple austerities of Kṛṣṇa conscious life, and they are never to be abandoned, even at the higher stages. Exalted Vaiṣṇavas—like Haridāsa Ṭhākura, the Six Gosvāmīs of Vṛndāvana, and Śrī Caitanya Mahāprabhu Himself—never gave up the basic spiritual practices. Pure devotional service in its progressive stages is like a ripening mango. The beginning of devotional service, if the devotional principles are taken up strictly, is pure devotional service, even though it is not fully mature. This is like a green mango; the full sweet mango taste is not present yet. But it is still a mango. So the only difference between the neophyte and the advanced is that the neophyte practices devotional principles out of duty and the advanced devotee does so in spontaneous love and full realization.

We have been discussing Vaiṣṇava behavior and stressing that a devotee's activities must not be superficial or hypocritical but up to the genuine standard. We think, therefore, that it is important to point out the most essential rules and regulations of spiritual life to consider once again the symptoms of one who is truly living as a devotee.

LIVING WITH DEVOTEES

One of the most important principles of Vaiṣṇava behavior is that one should perform devotional service in the association of devotees and never give this up under any circumstance.

> My dear highly glorified Lord, if one, in the association of pure devotees, hear even once the glories of Your activities, he does not, unless he is nothing but an

animal, give up the association of devotees, for no intelligent person would be so careless as to leave their association.

—*Bhāg.* 4.20.26

As living beings, we need engagement, and we need some form of society. Going into perpetual seclusion or silent meditation is not recommended, and it is almost impossible for most persons. Therefore, we should take up the right engagement, devotional service, and in the right company, the association of devotees. His Divine Grace Śrīla Prabhupāda created the International Society for Krishna Consciousness with the intention of providing centers and communities for people to come and hear and chant about Kṛṣṇa and live together in devotional service.

In former ages, devotees like Dhruva Mahārāja were ordered to perform austerities in the forest, but that is not congenial or recommended for the people of Kali-yuga. By the mercy of Lord Caitanya, devotional service has been made easy. Of course, the principles must still be followed, and that is best done by serving in the company of other devotees who are avoiding illicit sex, meat-eating, intoxication, and gambling—in a society where there is constant chanting of the holy name and rendering of devotional service. In this way, devotees live together harmoniously, and they transcend the limited identity of time and space. Śrīla Prabhupāda writes, "If the members of the International Society for Krishna Consciousness, putting faith in Kṛṣṇa as the center, live in harmony according to the order and principles of *Bhagavad-gītā*, then they are living in Vaikuṇṭha, not in this material world." (*Bhāg.* 3.15.33, purport)

One may say that he has tried living in the association of devotees but that the situation is not always exactly like Vaikuṇṭha. This is understandable, because the Kṛṣṇa consciousness movement is recruiting devotees from among the conditioned souls and because the movement exists amidst opposing forces within the world of *māyā*. Yet the association of devotees remains the only solace for one aspiring to serve Kṛṣṇa and go back to Godhead.

One of Śrīla Prabhupāda's most memorable statements, spoken during his last days on earth, was his request that his followers cooperate among themselves. "Your love for me will be shown," he said, "by how much you cooperate to keep this institution together after I am gone." Not only in his last days, but also during all his days as founder-*ācārya* of ISKCON, Śrīla Prabhupāda was promoting cooperation among the members. He acknowledged that individuals would sometimes differ, but it should not cause disruption. "I know the fight spirit is there in you Westerners," he wrote in a letter, "even if you do not care to fight, someone will induce you to fight." (Letter, November 13, 1975 to Alanātha dāsa)

Occasionally, a group of devotees would want to force an errant devotee out of the temple community, but Śrīla Prabhupāda would usually object, unless the fallen devotee was unredeemable. He asked his disciples to stick together, not out of material sentiment, but by keeping the order of the spiritual master in the center of their lives. The devotees should address each other as *prabhu* (master), and they should serve the leader of the masters, Prabhupāda. If the *prabhus* were actually surrendered to Prabhupāda, would they break off and go away?

Śrīla Prabhupāda compared the fighting of disciples to the fighting of sons who ultimately cause pain to the father. He told the story of the father who came home at night after a hard day's work and requested his sons to massage different parts of his body. But while the sons were massaging, they fell to quarreling with one another and began punching the different parts of his body. "By your fighting you are killing me!" the father cried out. And so also did Prabhupāda cry out: the inevitable quarreling should not become a painful situation for the spiritual master. "We must exist on cooperation," wrote Śrīla Prabhupāda, "otherwise the whole thing is doomed if we simply go on fighting over some small thing." (Letter, November 18, 1972 to Madhumaṅgala dāsa)

A neophyte disciple soon sees the practical realities of spiritual life, such as occasional quarreling among devotees. But if he becomes too disappointed at seeing imperfections, that may become a cause for falldown. It should be understood that the Kṛṣṇa consciousness movement is a sample of the spiritual world, but it is not yet perfect, since its individual members are still undergoing purification. Yet because Kṛṣṇa consciousness is a purificatory process, all devotees are on the right path for purification, and they should not be criticized unduly for faults that they are still maintaining. Once an initiated disciple left the association of devotees and wrote to Prabhupāda that she had done so because of the devotees' imperfections. Prabhupāda's reply exposed her greater defect in leaving.

> Just because some body has made some mistakes does that mean you should give up your whole career in Krsna Consciousness? What will that accomplish? Simply more rebirth and death. The fact that you have left our movement just on account of some minor disagreements shows that you are not actually serious about going back to home, back to Godhead. I suggest

> that you become serious about spiritual life and try to overlook the minor offenses of others.
>
> —Letter, March 14, 1975 to Banutanaya dāsī

THE MORNING PROGRAM

It begins with rising early for *maṅgala-ārati.* You have to. It may seem difficult at first. Because *maṅgala-ārati* occurs very early in the morning, one may prefer to sleep; but this is one of the simple austerities we must perform in this age when most of the austerities performed in previous ages are no longer possible. Lord Caitanya Mahāprabhu has given lenient directions for spiritual life in this age, but candidates for Kṛṣṇa consciousness must be determined to follow whatever He and His representative have asked us to do. Compared to the austerities of previous *yogīs* and devotees, our austerities are insignificant. But if we neglect our simple, required duties, then we cannot be successful in the most important mission of our human life.

In the *Kṛṣṇa* book Śrīla Prabhupāda describes how the young students in the *gurukula* practice the austerity of rising early at the bidding of the spiritual master. When a bell is sounded in the temple, they immediately rise, "and after finishing their morning duties, they sit down to study the *Vedas* or chant Vedic *mantras.*" Early rising and obedience to the *guru* are a basic regulative duty. This is described in *The Nectar of Devotion.*

> One has to follow these different regulative principles by the order of the spiritual master or on the strength of authoritative scriptures, and there can be no question of refusal. . . . For example, a person engaged in devotional service may be ordered to rise early in the morning and offer *ārati,* which is a form of Deity worship. In the beginning, by the order of his spiritual

master, one rises early in the morning and offers *ārati*, but then he develops real attachment.
—*Bhakti-rasāmṛta-sindhu* pgs. 21–22

By practicing the regulative principles, a devotee will awaken his original, natural love of Kṛṣṇa. The love is already there in one's heart, but it is the gift of the regulative practice that that love manifests. *Bhakti-yoga* is a science, and the devotee must proceed step by step to reach the higher stages. By practicing the regulative principles, we lose our desire for sinful habits; this leads us to firm conviction and then to the stages just prior to spontaneous love of God. Śrīla Prabhupāda and the previous *ācāryas* were fully aware of this scientific nature of *bhakti-yoga*; therefore, they did not recommend any compromise in a daily program that begins with early rising and *maṅgala-ārati*. If Śrīla Prabhupāda had compromised on some important points of regulative practice, he might have made or retained more followers, but that was not his interest. He was interested in creating first-class persons, genuine devotees of Kṛṣṇa, because only the devotee can actually attain love of God and distribute it to others. Even if there is only one pure devotee in the world, Śrīla Prabhupāda used to say, he can do great good for others. Therefore, Śrīla Prabhupāda instructed his temple managers to maintain the morning program as a prime responsibility.

Everything is done in conformity to a regular standard. For example, all the temple members, without exception must rise by 4:AM and attend mangala arati. Everyone living in the temple must agree to the standard by proper understanding of the philosophy of *tapasya*. We cannot expect our guests to follow all our principles, but whoever lives in the temple must follow.
—Letter, January 12, 1974 to Mukunda dāsa

CHANTING SIXTEEN ROUNDS

When Haridāsa Ṭhākura was old and was no longer able to chant his daily quota of 300,000 holy names, Lord Caitanya Mahāprabhu came to visit him and asked, "Can you ascertain what your disease is?" Haridāsa Ṭhākura replied, "My disease is that I cannot complete my rounds." (Cc. *Antya* 11.23) Śrīla Prabhupāda comments: "If one cannot complete the fixed number of rounds he is assigned he should be considered to be in a diseased condition of spiritual life . . . In our Kṛṣṇa consciousness movement we have fixed sixteen rounds as the minimum so that Westerners will not feel burdened."

Chanting sixteen rounds is the most basic and important of all the instructions of the spiritual master. To neglect this order is like committing spiritual suicide. At the time of initiation, a devotee promises to chant sixteen rounds daily and to follow the regulations. And in reciprocation, Lord Kṛṣṇa, acting through the spiritual master, relieves the new devotee of all his karmic reactions. The obligation for the disciple to keep his promise is a grave one, and often Śrīla Prabhupāda would remind his temple managers of this, especially when Prabhupāda was granting initiations.

> All initiated devotees must chant at least 16 rounds daily, without fail. Now that they are initiated there is no question of not doing their rounds. In court when a person swears to tell the truth he can be punished by perjury if he does not take it seriously and tells a lie, so those who will promise before the deity to follow the rules and regulations of initiated disciples will be punished if they fail to do so.
>
> —Letter, March 24, 1974 to Dayānanda dāsa

Sometimes a devotee takes on the sixteen-round quota in earnest but later rationalizes that he has become too busy in Kṛṣṇa's service and has no time to chant the minimum rounds. He may even imagine that his spiritual master has given him permission to do this and that by so working he is demonstrating advancement as a Kṛṣṇa conscious preacher. But Śrīla Prabhupāda refutes this bad logic: "We have witnessed that some of our contemporaries who are supposed to be great preachers have gradually fallen into the material conception of life because they have failed to chant the holy name of the Lord." (*Upadeśamṛta* #5)

People also speculate as to why sixteen rounds have been chosen as a minimum. They sometimes remark that the number seems arbitrary and that there is no absolute obligation to chant that much. But Śrīla Prabhupāda, as the authorized spiritual master for establishing Kṛṣṇa consciousness, very deliberately arrived at sixteen as the absolute minimum number of rounds daily for his disciples. Śrīla Prabhupāda's spiritual master asked his disciples to chant sixty-four rounds, but Śrīla Prabhupāda experienced that that was not possible for the restless Westerners. His choice of sixteen rounds as a rock-bottom minimum is not a whimsical thing of a number that can be lowered as one likes.

Once Śrīla Prabhupāda was informed by mail that one of his temple presidents was chanting only fourteen rounds daily. Śrīla Prabhupāda replied simply that he should be encouraged to chant his sixteen rounds. "The injunction is *kirtaniya sada hari,*" wrote Śrīla Prabhupāda. "One should always be chanting all day. The 16 rounds is just a minimum I set for my disciples so that they would chant at least that much." (Letter, June 25, 1974 to Jagadīśa dāsa)

When Śrīla Prabhupāda first visited Japan in 1970, several young people became his admirers and took up the chanting of Hare Kṛṣṇa. Two of them wrote to Śrīla Prabhupāda and told him that they were experiencing joy while chanting the *mahā-mantra*. This news pleased Śrīla Prabhupāda, and he replied with the ecstatic advice that they should "chant constantly."

> Please therefore continue to chant this mantra as many times as possible throughout the day and night. I do not think there is any inconvenience or loss on your part if you do so all the time. Even when you are walking, you can softly chant Hare Krishna, Hare Krishna, or even when you are on the bus going to somewhere you can also chant. When you are working with your hands you can also chant, and when you are resting or going to take rest you can also chant. Even in your toilet room while taking bath you can also chant. In this way there is no limitation or restriction for chanting this Holy Name of God, Krishna, and His Energy, Hara. In doing this business there is no loss, but there is a very great gain which is transcendental realization.
>
> —Letter, April 22, 1970 to Minoru & Kenji

Exclusive chanting on beads is not our only duty. Not only are we too restless, but we have many duties to perform on behalf of the Kṛṣṇa consciousness movement. But all devotees must chant the minimum rounds, no matter what else they have to do. "Amongst all our duties we must never forget to complete our sixteen rounds," Śrīla Prabhupāda wrote to a disciple who had raised some questions about the *mantra*. "We should not be carried away simply by the Krishna duties which are also regarded as good as chanting, but in all circumstances we shall not forget this duty." (Letter, January 24, 1970 to Ranadira dāsa)

There should be no doubt or speculation in this matter, since Śrīla Prabhupāda has made this instruction sufficiently clear through numerous writings, many of which stress the chanting of Hare Kṛṣṇa as the most important of all duties.

> One may have other duties to perform under the direction of the spiritual master, but he must first abide by the spiritual master's order to chant a certain number of rounds. In our Kṛṣṇa consciousness movement we have recommended that the neophyte chant at least sixteen rounds. This chanting of sixteen rounds is absolutely necessary if one wants to remember Kṛṣṇa and not forget Him. Of all the regulative principles, the spiritual master's order to chant at least sixteen rounds is most essential.
>
> —Cc. *Madhya* 22.113

The vow to chant sixteen rounds must always be completed, every day. Yet we may ask, "What if there is some extraordinary circumstance and I somehow don't finish the sixteen rounds in a day?" In *The Nectar of Devotion* Śrīla Prabhupāda deals with this unlikely event: "If one is not even able to chant sixteen rounds, then he must make it up the next day. He must be sure to keep his vow. If he does not strictly follow this out, then he is sure to be negligent. That is offensive in the service of the Lord." (*Bhakti-rasāmṛta-sindhu* pg. 63) There is no mention of the concocted practice of storing up unfinished rounds until one is hundreds of rounds "in debt" and weeks behind in maintaining his vow. Such things are the products of fertile imaginations and are not approved, standard behavior.

What is the position of a devotee who consistently fails to chant the prescribed sixteen rounds? This question was asked to Śrīla Prabhupāda on a morning walk and he replied, "He is an animal." But then what to do with the "animal"? On another occasion, several devotees went to Śrīla Prabhupāda to report that one of the society's highly placed *sannyāsīs* was not regularly chanting his rounds. When they inquired what should be done, Śrīla Prabhupāda replied that they should approach the *sannyāsī* with straws in their mouths (as a sign of humility) and, falling at his feet, beg him to please chant his sixteen rounds. Once, a temple leader wrote to Śrīla Prabhupāda that some of the Indian trustees of the temple corporation were not following all the principles or chanting sixteen rounds. Śrīla Prabhupāda said that these were important men and should be dealt with tactfully so that they would not be offended. But "they should be induced by the other trustees who are following, to step down." (Letter, January 17, 1976 to Madhudviṣa dāsa)

In other words, devotees should be tolerant of an incidental failure to follow all the principles. Everyone is prone to make mistakes; if offenses are not excused, then who among us is qualified? But when the failures are serious and persistent, we must be decisive. "That tolerant attitude must be there to a certain extent," Śrīla Prabhupāda wrote to a temple president, "but we must remain also always firm on this point, that the brahmacaris living in the temple should not disobey the orders of the spiritual master." (Letter, December 29, 1972 to Cyavana)

HEARING SRIMAD-BHĀGAVATAM

The morning program is a power-packed succession of the most beneficial devotional practices. By taking part attentively in *maṅgala-ārati, kīrtana, tulasī-ārati, japa, guru-pūjā,* Deity worship, and *Śrīmad-Bhāgavatam* class, a devotee is sure to stimulate his original, ecstatic love of God, which has long been covered by *māyā*. All the senses, the mind, and the intelligence are cleansed of material conceptions, and one comes to see Kṛṣṇa face to face—with the eyes, with the heart, and with the intellect. One must attend the program not only physically but mentally. A devotee must make the mind his friend and bring it under the control of the intelligence by careful chanting, hearing, and remembering. If a person drags himself through the program reluctantly and allows himself to remain sleepy (in the mode of ignorance), he will not be able to fully derive the strength and purification that is easily available if one is attentive.

Bhaktivinoda Ṭhākura describes the feelings of Kṛṣṇa *prema* which are obtainable by participation in even the simplest parts of the morning observances.

> When I hear the sound of the *mṛdaṅga,* in my heart I always desire to join in *kīrtana,* and when I hear the bona fide songs describing Lord Caitanya's pastimes, my heart dances in ecstasy . . . When I take *caraṇāmṛta* of the Deity I see the holy Ganges water that comes from the feet of Lord Viṣṇu, and my bliss knows no bounds. By seeing the *tulasī* tree my heart feels joy, and Lord Mādhava is also satisfied.
>
> —*Śuddha-bhakata* by Śrīla Bhaktivinoda Ṭhākura

Why should a temple leader have to nag and coerce reluctant persons to take part in such blissful morning practices? He shouldn't. Therefore, unless a person rises early and attends the morning program, he shouldn't live in a temple. In writing to one temple president, Śrīla Prabhupāda asserted that attendance at *maṅgala-ārati* and chanting of sixteen rounds were the most important points of the Kṛṣṇa conscious process. "But make it so that people may not think it too repressive so they will not go away, impressive but not repressive, that is the system." (Letter, February 13, 1972 to Hayagrīva dāsa)

The morning program will be impressive if the temple leaders themselves are strictly participating and are also feeling some of the happy mood of Bhaktivinoda Ṭhākura, then they can better inspire the others to follow. But if despite good example and precept, someone doesn't care to participate in the most required morning practices, then that person is unfit to live in the temple. In an anxiety to recruit new, full-time members, the temple authorities should not bring in persons who are not advanced enough to voluntarily attend the morning program.

> Of course we work very very hard just to get someone to come to the platform of a devotee of Krsna, so we shall not be too much hasty to drive anyone out. Therefore we may forgive once, twice, but more than that we must take other steps. So if any new candidate for devotee comes forward you may test him very thoroughly to understand from him if he is ready to accept our strict standard of temple living. Let him understand that it is not an arbitrary or whimsical decision on our parts to become like military camp, rather we are strictly adhering to our devotional principles only so that we may make advancement in Kṛṣṇa consciousness and be protected from the attack of māyā consciousness.
>
> —Letter, December 31, 1972 to Dhanañjaya dāsa

At the heart of the morning program is the recitation and lecture from *Śrīmad-Bhāgavatam*. Hearing from *Śrīmad-Bhāgavatam* is an eternal process, and on this planet it has been going on for at least 5,000 years, ever since Śukadeva Gosvāmī explained it to Mahārāja Parīkṣit. But the specific format of the *Śrīmad-Bhāgavatam* class that devotees in the Kṛṣṇa consciousness movement follow was introduced by Śrīla Prabhupāda.

> I am very much stressing at this point that all of my students shall be very much conversant with the philosophy of Krishna Consciousness, and that they should read out books very diligently at least one or two hours daily and try to understand the subject matter from varieties of angles. We are holding morning class her at Los Angeles in the temple and I am speaking from 7 to 8 a.m. , and the process is that we are going through some chapters of Srimad-Bhagavatam by taking one sloka each day, and reading the sanskrit aloud, each word is pronounced by me and repeated by the students and then altogether we chant the slokas several times until we have learned it. And then we discuss subject matter very minutely and inspect it from all angles of approach and savor the new understandings. So you introduce this new system in all centers in your zone, and you will discover that everyone becomes very much enlivened by these daily classes. Read one sloka and discuss then go on to the next sloka on the next day, and so on, and even if you discuss one verse each day it will take you 50 years to finish Srimad-Bhagavatam in this way. So we have got ample stock of acquiring knowledge. And if the students get knowledge more and more, they will automatically become convinced and very easily perform their duties for tapasya or renunciation of the material bondage, that will be their successful advancement in Krishna Consciousness.
>
> —Letter, June 16, 1972 to Madhudviṣa dāsa

As Prabhupāda introduced a specific form for the *Śrīmad-Bhāgavatam* class, he also stressed the importance of his devotees' thoroughly learning the Vaiṣṇava philosophy. Prabhupāda wrote to one of his *sannyāsīs*:

> It is better to maintain a devotee than to try to convince others to become a devotee. . . . Your first job should be to make sure that every one of the devotees in your zone of management is reading regularly our literatures and discussing the subject matter seriously from different angles of seeing, and that they are somehow or other absorbing the knowledge of Kṛṣṇa Conscious philosophy. . . . What good are many, many devotees if none of them are knowledgeable?
>
> —Letter, June 16, 1972 to Satsvarūpa dāsa Goswami

Hearing *Śrīmad-Bhāgavatam* regularly is of crucial importance to every devotee. The spiritual benefits cannot be overestimated, and they are glorified in all the scriptures. Somehow or other, if a devotee misses hearing *Śrīmad-Bhāgavatam,* then he misses the greatest opportunity that comes with the human form of life. Simply by submissively hearing the Vedic knowledge, the *bhakti-yogī* surpasses all other forms of meditation. Yet this hearing should not be an occasional diversion; it should be regular, constant.

Kṛṣṇadāsa Kavirāja compares hearing to eating and drinking. If an ordinary man does not eat, he will grow weak and die. Similarly, if a devotee doesn't taste the transcendental pastimes of Lord Caitanya Mahāprabhu and Lord Kṛṣṇa, he will gradually weaken and die spiritually. To hear an authorized speaker elucidate a verse from *Śrīmad-Bhāgavatam* is *bhakti-yoga.* "To hear and explain them [the Vedic literatures] is more important than reading them," writes Śrīla Prabhupāda. "One can assimilate the knowledge of the revealed scriptures only by hearing and explaining." (*Bhāg.* 1.1.6, purport) If we had only the translated verses of *Bhagavad-gītā* and *Śrīmad-Bhāgavatam,* without the authorized purports, we would not be able to grasp the real meaning.

This brings us back to our main thesis in *Vaiṣṇava Behavior*: it is the devotee himself who best demonstrates Kṛṣṇa conscious knowledge and realization. The *Śrīmad-Bhāgavatam* class is an opportunity to experience the Vaiṣṇava philosophy in dynamic exchange, as the speaker explains the verses and answers relevant questions. Even though we are small and humble devotees, compared to the great *ācāryas* of the past, if we faithfully repeat the message and hear with intelligence and submission, then the potency will be intact. And the *Śrīmad-Bhāgavatam* knowledge is so comprehensive that all "new" questions and problems of the modern day can be sufficiently solved through the light of the *Bhāgavatam.*

The Kṛṣṇa consciousness process is based on philosophy; it is not sentimental or invented by upstarts. Self-proclaimed incarnations of God sometimes foolishly declare that there is no need for scriptures or books and that they will simply bless us with their own perfection. But this kind of crazy talk should be rejected. The spiritual master or any Kṛṣṇa conscious person, receives knowledge from the original speaker of the scriptures, Śrīla Vyāsadeva, through his disciplic succession. Those who aspire to be genuine devotees are, therefore, always serious and eager to hear *Śrīmad-Bhāgavatam* so that they may fix themselves in steady Kṛṣṇa consciousness.

Another foolish proposal against the regular hearing of *Śrīmad-Bhāgavatam* is put forward by the *prākṛta-sahajiyās,* or the pseudodevotees who take devotional service cheaply. "Sometimes they give a theatrical performance," writes Śrīla Prabhupāda, "and cry for the Lord with tears in their eyes. Of course, all scriptural conclusions are washed off by these tears." (Cc. *Madhya* 1.34, purport) *Prākṛta-sahajiyās* sometimes criticize the literary disciples of Lord Caitanya, such as Jīva

Gosvāmī, thinking them to be dry speculators for compiling big books of Vaiṣṇava conclusions. But actually the books of the Gosvāmīs are never speculative; they are filled with valuable *kṛṣṇa-kathā* and strong arguments against Māyāvāda speculations. By hearing *Śrīmad-Bhāgavatam*, a devotee avoids both dry speculation and sentimental fanaticism.

Religion nowadays is often regarded as superstitious and dogmatic. Biblical accounts are sometimes incomplete, because the people to whom the Bible was spoken were of lower classes and could not understand the higher conclusions. Therefore, people have traditionally had to accept the teachings of the Bible on faith. But, in the modern age, facilities for education have expanded widely, and people have more access to philosophical and scientific information. Consequently, it is no longer sufficient to tell people to accept theism simply on blind faith and dogma. But people are being misled by atheistic science and mental speculation, and they have many questions to ask—questions that must be met with philosophical replies if people are to become satisfied in transcendental knowledge. Therefore, the world needs the *Śrīmad-Bhāgavatam*. The *Śrīmad-Bhāgavatam* gives an especially clear and complete philosophical presentation of the Absolute Truth. Śrīla Prabhupāda writes:

> By a careful reading [of *Śrīmad-Bhāgavatam*] one will know God perfectly well, so much so that the reader will be sufficiently educated to defend himself from the onslaught of atheists. Over and above this, the reader will be able to convert others to accepting God as a concrete principle.
>
> —Preface to *Śrīmad-Bhāgavatam*

A reluctant devotee may complain and give excuses for why he does not regularly attend the *Bhāgavatam* class, but I will not attempt here to suggest various persuasive methods of convincing devotees to do what the ISKCON founder-*ācārya* has already instructed them to do. In the early days of ISKCON at 26 Second Avenue, Śrīla Prabhupāda said that each devotee should wash his own plate after taking *prasādam*. One of the disciples complained to Śrīla Prabhupāda that the devotees were neglecting their duty and simply piling the plates in the sink. "Could you tell us something, Swamiji, to get the devotees to do what they're supposed to do?" Śrīla Prabhupāda replied, " The order of the spiritual master is sufficient."

A DEVOTEE IS FULLY ENGAGED

After participating in the full morning program and after honoring breakfast *prasādam*, a devotee should be ready to perform a full day's work at his devotional occupation. Devotional service is meant to totally engage a person—body, mind, and speech—in the service of the Lord. The *Bhāgavatam* declares that devotional service "must be unmotivated and uninterrupted to completely satisfy the self." (*Bhāg.* 1.2.6) A Vaiṣṇava is not a lazy fellow or a part-time religionist. Because he has at least a partial understanding that Lord Kṛṣṇa is the all-attractive Supreme Personality of Godhead and that the only goal of life is to satisfy Him, a Vaiṣṇava cannot turn away from Kṛṣṇa after a show of morning worship and go do "something else."

There *is* nothing else but Kṛṣṇa. Or rather, there is Kṛṣṇa and His illusory energy *māyā*. A devotee avoids the clutches of *māyā* and the resultant sufferings of material life by fully absorbing himself in some form of authorized devotional service. "Seekers of the Absolute Truth are never lured by unnecessary engagement in sense gratification," writes Śrīla Prabhupāda, "because the serious students seeking the Absolute Truth are always overwhelmed with the work of researching the Truth." (*Bhāg*. 1.2.10, purport) When a disciple wrote to Śrīla Prabhupāda confessing that she was confused, Śrīla Prabhupāda recommended that she go on chanting but remain fully engaged in devotional work. "So you have sufficient engagement there?" he asked in his return letter. "Because if we are not fulltime engaged then the mind is free to do its fickle business of rejection and acceptance for sense gratification. Maya will immediately enter—we do not even have to call her—the moment we are not absorbed in Kṛṣṇa's devotional service." (Letter, July 20, 1973 to Govinda dāsī)

The varieties of devotional service are endless. They are dictated by one's personal preference and by the priorities set by the spiritual master. Śrīla Prabhupāda used to say, "Do the needful," meaning do what is required to carry out the desires of the spiritual master. Sometimes the needful may be to collect donations for building a temple, or it may be to approach city officials to get a permit for the Ratha-yātrā festival. The needful may mean comparing the prices of different printers for the best bargain in printing the spiritual master's books. Or it may mean a *gṛhastha* should go out and get a job. It may mean anything, according to time and place. Spiritual activities are not stereotyped, nor should they be confused with material activities. Based on the confirmation of Rūpa Gosvāmī, a devotee knows that although the material world is full of misery, it is also spiritual because the devotee can engage everything in the service of Kṛṣṇa.

The activities of an advanced Vaiṣṇava are inconceivable. He is always thinking of Kṛṣṇa and he knows the art of how to engage everything in Kṛṣṇa's service. When Śrīla Prabhupāda was attempting to single-handedly publish his first volumes of *Śrīmad-Bhāgavatam* in India, he noticed that some of the nondevotees were puzzled about his activities. Śrīla Prabhupāda wrote about this in the preface to his second volume of *Śrīmad-Bhāgavatam,* "They see that we are moving in the cities, in the government office, banks and other business places for promoting the publication of *Śrīmad-Bhāgavatam*. They also see that we are moving in the press, paper market and amongst the book binders also, away from our residence of Vṛndāvana, and they conclude sometimes, mistakenly, that we are also doing the same business in the dress of a mendicant!"

Great kings like Mahārāja Yudhiṣṭhira and Mahārāja Parīkṣit ruled the citizens on behalf of Lord Kṛṣṇa, and warriors like Arjuna and Hanumān fought to satisfy the desires of the Supreme Lord. Vaiṣṇava scholars like Jīva Gosvāmī and Baladeva Vidyabhūṣaṇa wrote highly intellectual works to establish the transcendental position of the Supreme Personality of Godhead, and poets like Jayadeva Gosvāmī and Bhaktivinoda Ṭhākura wrote poems and songs for the pleasure of the Lord and Vaiṣṇavas. A woman like Queen Kuntī raised her children as her Kṛṣṇa conscious duty, and Gāndhārī followed her husband through all the difficult days of his checkered life. Ideal preachers like Lord Caitanya Mahāprabhu and Lord Nityānanda traveled to spread Kṛṣṇa consciousness to scholars and to the common people and devotees like the Kurma *brāhmana* stayed at home. And all these varied activities continue to go on up to the present day, carried out by sincere devotees working under the expert orders of Vaiṣṇava *ācāryas*.

The list of services to Kṛṣṇa can be extended on and on, as all the latest inventions of technology, such as high-speed jet transport and high-tech computers, become utilized by intelligent servants of Kṛṣṇa for spreading the mission of Kṛṣṇa consciousness. No one willing to work can complain of unemployment in the service of the Lord. And as soon as one becomes unemployed in devotional service *māyā* employs him by force.

The morning program of chanting and hearing is dynamically interrelated with a devotee's occupational duties. From the morning *sādhana*, the devotee gets the spiritual fortitude to carry on throughout the day, executing laborious service on behalf of the spiritual master. And by working with his senses throughout the day, the devotee earns the pleasure of Kṛṣṇa, who then increases the devotee's taste for chanting and hearing about Him. Both regulated worship and preaching must be prosecuted according to a healthy balance.

No one should make devotional service an excuse not to work. When Śrīla Prabhupāda heard a devotee was taking all day to finish her sixteen rounds, he replied, "She must do some duty. Sometimes it is given as a plea to avoid doing more active service." As a devotee cannot excuse himself from the morning program, similarly, he cannot excuse himself from engaging in a full day's service on behalf of Kṛṣṇa. "In the temples and monasteries," wrote Śrīla Prabhupāda, "gatherings of unnecessary, rejected, lazy fellows should be strictly disallowed." (*Bhāg*. 7.13.8, purport) Whether one lives in the temple or in his home, whether one is employed directly in the preaching or is working outside to earn a living, if one wants to become an honest devotee, he has to fully engage himself in a worthwhile service that is acceptable to Kṛṣṇa.

AVOIDING SINFUL ACTIVITIES

Pure devotional service grants the devotee the power to break the chain of sinful activities in which all souls are suffering within the material world. A conditioned soul suffers due to his past sinful acts, and future suffering also awaits him for present sinful acts. But devotional service secures the special mercy of the Supreme Lord, Śrī Kṛṣṇa, who promises to protect the surrendered devotee from all his past and future sinful reactions. This benediction one could never achieve on his own, even after hundreds of years of pious activities and acts of atonement. And yet, relief from sin is only a beginning installment of the rewards of devotional service, which ultimately leads on to the eternal life of bliss and knowledge in the spiritual world with Kṛṣṇa.

When we consider how almost all human beings in the present age of Kali are very prone to sinful acts, and when we consider how these acts condemn one to repeated birth and death, then we can perceive that the devotee is certainly the recipient of inconceivable mercy. Lord Caitanya Mahāprabhu expressed this when he welcomed Sanātana Gosvāmī to become His disciple. "Kṛṣṇa has saved you from Mahāraurava, life's deepest hell. He is an ocean of mercy and His activities are very grave." (Cc. *Madhya* 20.63)

The devotee's good fortune is due to the causeless mercy of Kṛṣṇa and the spiritual master. This mercy is extended to all souls in the human form of life, but only the fortunate—those who accept Lord Kṛṣṇa and His representative as their saviors—become picked up from the ocean of sins and suffering. Why this great fortune is bestowed on some and not others may be partially attributed to *karma*. And yet with or without past pious acts, Kṛṣṇa bestows His benedictions as He pleases, out of His causeless, inconceivable mercy.

Although the present age is most sinful, it has a most merciful feature. In Kali-yuga the Supreme Personality of Godhead, Lord Caitanya, expands His mercy to the fallen. Lord Caitanya offers an easy method—chanting and hearing the holy names—which alone is powerful enough to free a sinful person from more sins than he could ever commit.

The definition of sin is clear: disobedience against the laws of God. But the age is so dark in ignorance that people defiantly deny that there is even such a thing as sin. Their defiant disobedience is itself the essence of sin. For example, it is not that sex life is itself sinful, but when it is indulged in without restriction and with no sense of using it in service to God, then it is. Similarly, although eating is not sinful, meat-eating is sinful. Kṛṣṇa has provided full facility for progressive and happy human life with religious sex and with sumptuous provision of food. If a human being fulfills his desires without breaking the laws of God, then there is no sin for him, and he becomes eligible for higher spiritual understanding. But when people are godless, they wantonly kill innocent and valuable animals like the cow, simply to gratify the tongue. They do not consider God's will. And as the age of godlessness increases, all remnants of morality will disappear, until people will eat the flesh of their own family members and—as they are already doing—engage in sex acts with less discrimination than the hogs and dogs.

In previous chapters we have discussed how the devotee endeavors to free himself from material implication by engaging in the transcendental service of the Lord, Śrī Kṛṣṇa. Thus service begins with submissive hearing of the philosophy of spiritual life as spoken by Kṛṣṇa's representative. When a devotee becomes fixed in the conception of self-realization and devotional service, he goes beyond working only for his own salvation and becomes inspired by the mission of the great *ācāryas* within this world—to give freedom from death to all people.

Now let us discuss why and how a Vaiṣṇava avoids sinful activities. A devotee is one who has recovered his intelligence and sanity. Thus he avoids sin, just as an intelligent child or sane person avoids touching fire. "A devotee is nevertheless always alert not to commit any sinful activities," states Śrīla Prabhupāda in *The Nectar of Devotion*, "this is his specific qualification as a devotee." The Vaiṣṇava's strictness against committing sinful activities is another sense in which devotional service is beyond sentimental of sham religion. The devotee does not cry out God's name while continuing to defy His laws. An honest devotee is not such a hypocrite or blasphemer of God's mercy. In the beginning, when a neophyte is first entering devotional service, he may retain some of his bad habits, but Lord Kṛṣṇa clearly states in *Bhagavad-gītā* that He overlooks such residual tendencies. Anyone who has resolved to serve and worship Lord Kṛṣṇa as the Supreme Personality of Godhead is already a devotee, and Kṛṣṇa will protect him, even if there are discrepancies due to past bad habits. Whatever was done in the past will not be held against the devotee, but from the time he accepts initiation from an authorized spiritual master, Kṛṣṇa relieves him from his sinful reactions—from then on he must very strictly avoid sinful acts. The vow taken at initiation, therefore, consists of four "do nots": no illicit sex, no intoxication, no meat-eating, and no gambling. The basic vow also includes the main "do": always chant at least sixteen rounds of the Hare Kṛṣṇa *mantra* daily.

These four prohibitions and one positive principle will enable a devotee to stay clear of all vicious *karma*.

But what happens if a devotee is initiated and afterwards feels an urge for sinful activity? What is that urge, and how can he overcome it? The urge for sin is the contamination of the false ego (*ahaṅkāra*). Due to false ego a conditioned soul thinks that he is the center and enjoyer of existence; therefore, he is not inclined to be restrained by God's law. He does not like to be God's servant or the servant of God's servant. This means the bewildered soul has forgotten his identity, just like a madman or a person delirious with a fever. As to how the pure spirit soul contacts the false ego, that is due to the misuse of his free will. Devotional service can correct all these anomalies, provided one stays tightly at the lotus feet of the spiritual master and goes on hearing from him and serving his order. Thus the conditioned soul will retain his original spiritual intelligence, free of false ego.

The false ego first contaminates the intelligence and then the mind and senses. The conditioned soul then thinks of himself as the enjoyer of the world of matter, forgetting that his real self-satisfaction can be had only in relation to Kṛṣṇa. This predicament of the spirit soul within the material world should be already known to the devotee, but if he is at a stage where his realization is only theoretical, he may again meditate on the possibilities of enjoying himself apart from Kṛṣṇa. At that point he again misuses his free will and becomes covered by false ego. In the beginning stages, therefore, before the devotee is completely fixed in the higher spiritual taste, he must avoid sinful life by the strength of *sādhana* (devotional acts based on duty). Just as on the order of the spiritual master the neophyte devotee rises early to worship the Deity, so on the order of the *guru* and *śāstra* he must also agree to restrain himself from sinful acts. It is as simple as that.

But devotional service is so purifying that very soon the devotee begins to experience a higher taste. In the *Bhagavad-gītā,* Lord Kṛṣṇa says that until one experiences a higher taste, his attempts to restrain himself from sin will be very precarious.

> The embodied soul may be restricted from sense enjoyment, though the taste for sense objects remains. But, ceasing such engagements by experiencing a higher taste, he is fixed in consciousness.
>
> —Bg. 2.60

It is a great wonder that Śrīla Prabhupāda's revolutionary movement has succeeded in the Western countries where sinful activities are accepted as normal. That this movement now has thousands of followers who are all abstaining from sinful activities is a testimony to the purity and power of devotional service. Śrīla Prabhupāda himself admitted that at first he had not expected such success. "In a country where everyone is trained from childhood to indulge in sinful activities," Prabhupāda remarked, "who will accept these restrictions, no meat, fish and eggs, no intoxicants, no gambling, and no illicit sex life. These things are the life and soul of the western people, and I never imagined that even one person would accept it. But by the mercy of my spiritual master and Krishna the thing has taken shape." (Letter, December 7, 1975 to Śivarāma dāsa)

But Śrīla Prabhupāda also experienced that some of his student suffered relapses, a phenomenon he explained by using the analogy of the bedbug. In the winter the bedbug appears to be only skin, but in the summer season it becomes fat with blood. Similarly, if a devotee only artificially renounces the world, then as soon as he finds the opportunity, he will again become materialistic. Becoming a pure devotee is not such an easy thing. It is not just a matter of putting on some saffron clothes and applying *tilaka*. Therefore, Lord Kṛṣṇa states in the *Bhagavad-gītā* that *māyā* can only be overcome by His grace.

> This divine energy of Mine, consisting of the three modes of material nature, is difficult to overcome. But those who have surrendered unto Me can easily cross beyond it.
>
> —Bg. 7.14

It is inevitable that, even if one becomes a devotee, he will sometimes be haunted by past material desires due to his previous contact with those desires. At such times the sincere devotee has no alternative but to stick to the regulative principles of chanting and behavior. If one develops the behavior described in this book and performs these practices, not superficially but with full surrender, then he will be able to avoid a relapse into sinful life. A devotee will no longer be affected by the pale attractions of sinful life when, by following the regulative devotional principles, he attains the stage of love of Kṛṣṇa.

The Twenty-six Qualities of a Devotee

Introduction

WHILE TEACHING Sanātana Gosvāmī, Lord Caitanya described twenty-six qualities of the Vaiṣṇava:

kṛpālu, akṛta-droha, satya-sāra, sama
nidoṣa, vadānya, mṛdu, śuci, akiñcana

sarvopakāraka, śānta, kṛṣṇaika-śaraṇa
akāma, anīha, sthira, vijita-ṣaḍ-guṇa

mita-bhuk, apramatta, mānada, amānī
gambhīra, karuṇa, maitra, kavi, dakṣa, maunī

Devotees are always merciful, humble, truthful, equal to all, faultless, magnanimous, mild and clean. They are without material possessions, and they perform welfare work for everyone. They are peaceful, surrendered to Kṛṣṇa and desireless. They are indifferent to material acquisitions and are fixed in devotional service. They completely control the six bad qualities—lust, anger, greed and so forth. They eat only as much as required, and they are not inebriated. They are respectful, grave, compassionate and without false prestige. They are friendly, poetic, expert and silent.

—Cc. *Madhya* 22.78–80

It is not, however, that a devotee must work separately to achieve each of these qualities. As Śukadeva Gosvāmī explains in *Śrīmad-Bhāgavatam*:

kecit kevalayā bhaktyā
vāsudeva-parāyaṇāḥ
aghaṁ dhunvanti kārtsnyena
nīhāram iva bhāskaraḥ

Only a rare person who has adopted complete, unalloyed devotional service to Kṛṣṇa can uproot the weeds of sinful actions with no possibility that they will revive. He can do this simply by discharging devotional service, just as the sun can immediately dissipate fog by its rays.

—*Bhāg.* 6.1.15

Just by executing pure devotional service a devotee attains all good qualities. In *Bhagavad-gītā* (13.8–12) Lord Kṛṣṇa mentions twenty items of knowledge. In the purport Prabhupāda explains unalloyed devotional service as the most important item: "If one takes to devotional service in full Kṛṣṇa consciousness, the other nineteen items automatically develop within him."

Prahlāda Mahārāja described devotional service as a ninefold process, beginning with chanting, hearing, and remembering the Lord. If we perform devotional service, we will automatically develop all the transcendental qualities. *Śrīmad-Bhāgavatam* states, therefore, that a devotee develops all the good qualities of the demigods. Control of the senses—which is very difficult even for the *yogīs*—comes very easily to the devotee because he engages his senses in the service of Kṛṣṇa. Monistic liberation seems hellish, and elevation to the heavenly planets is like a phantasmagoria to the devotee. Only devotional service is perfect and complete.

Then what is the point of Lord Caitanya's describing the devotee's twenty-six qualities? One reason is to show us the richness of the Vaiṣṇava's character. It is glorification of the Vaiṣṇava. Another reason is that we can see whether we are developing these qualities. Regarding the *Gītā's* twenty items of knowledge, Śrīla Prabhupāda writes, "As for actual advancement in spiritual science, one should have a test to see how far he is progressing. He can judge by these items."

By hearing how great devotees manifest these qualities, we can better understand transcendental culture. The Kṛṣṇa consciousness movement is meant to sweep over the world, and these twenty-six qualities, therefore must ultimately become the standard for all humanity. These qualities, beginning with mercifulness, must be understood in the transcendental sense, not as they would appear to an ordinary person.

Although the twenty-six qualities are not independent of devotional service, we may nevertheless strive to behave in devotional service so as to fulfill them all. To be a devotee means many things. For example, although it is important to preach, if one's behavior is not exemplary his preaching will be ineffective. Or, one may be very careful about cleanliness but not chant Hare Kṛṣṇa. There are many things a devotee must be accomplished in. All his qualities are sublime; no one can find any fault in him.

1

A devotee is merciful, kṛpālu.

Lord Kapila, in His teaching to His mother Devahūti, discusses mercifulness as one of the symptoms of a *sādhu*. Prabhupāda comments:

> He [the Vaiṣṇava] is merciful because he is the well-wisher of all living entities. He is not only a well-wisher of human society, but a well-wisher of the animal society as well. It is said here, *sarva dehinām*, which indicates all living entities who have accepted material bodies. Not only does the human being have a material body, but other living beings, such as cats and dogs, also have material bodies. The devotee of the Lord is merciful to everyone—the cats, dogs, trees, etc. He treats all living entities in such a way that they can ultimately get salvation from this material entanglement.
>
> —*Bhāg*. 3.25.21, purport

We may think, "Yes, Lord Caitanya and Śrīla Prabhupāda can be merciful, but how can I be merciful?" The answer is that by serving the merciful great soul and by serving his cause, we can act mercifully on his order. We can serve the merciful *mahātma*; therefore, we can share in his distribution of mercy. We can distribute Kṛṣṇa consciousness under the authorization of the merciful and compassionate great soul, and thus we also become merciful workers. A medic on the battlefield engaged in the menial task of bandaging the wounded may lack a deep feeling of mercy, but he is merciful nevertheless because his work is a mercy mission. He is compassionate, because he has enlisted in the cause of compassion. But mercifulness is best expressed not in tending simply to the bodily needs of others but in giving back them their eternal relationship with Kṛṣṇa. In fact, to give a person anything other than Kṛṣṇa consciousness is violence.

The principles of *bhāgavata-dharma* are merciful, and anyone who follows them automatically gives up all kinds of unkindness and its resultant *karma*. If we follow the Vedic codes of religion, then by obedience alone we will act on the platform of mercifulness to all living entities. We will not kill the innocent animals, and we will give the human beings Kṛṣṇa consciousness.

In describing the quality of mercy, I have done so exclusively in terms of Kṛṣṇa consciousness. And I will continue to describe each of the twenty-six qualities in this way. These are, after all, the qualities of a Vaiṣṇava, and nothing a Vaiṣṇava does is apart from Kṛṣṇa. Kṛṣṇa is everything for everyone, and the devotee knows this. Everything is under Kṛṣṇa's control and is part of His energy. One of Kṛṣṇa's energies is material, like the prison house, and the other is His superior energy, the transcendental nature. We are all spirit souls, and we are meant to live eternally in the blissful, spiritual energy. When I discuss each quality, therefore, I will do so in terms of that spiritual nature. We are not concerned here with material kindness, or the atheist's humility, or truthfulness without Kṛṣṇa. No. Everything must be understood in its relationship with Kṛṣṇa.

2

A devotee is not defiant, *akṛta-droha.**

Before meeting my spiritual master, Śrīla Prabhupāda, I used to think of humility as extremely elusive and mental; if one became humble, then wouldn't he be proud of his humility? It seemed more like an abstract game than a substantial reality. But now I have seen humility in Śrīla Prabhupāda and in the great Vaiṣṇava *ācāryas* of the past. In his *Śaraṇāgati,* Bhaktivinoda Ṭhākura evokes the attitude of humility in a way that is very helpful to devotees. Although Bhaktivinoda Ṭhākura is an empowered, liberated *ācārya,* he describes himself as one of the fallen conditioned souls, and thus he laments having wasted his life without Kṛṣṇa consciousness. He says that he is coming to Kṛṣṇa consciousness at the end of his life, not because of his own virtuous decision but because material life has ruined him and he now has no alternative. He is truly humiliated, forced by the vicissitudes of time and fate to be humble. Seeing "gloomy death approaching," finding himself unable to enjoy sense pleasures, he humbly harkens to the message of Lord Caitanya.

Bhaktivinoda Ṭhākura also expresses sadness that he did not surrender to Kṛṣṇa long before, and this sadness

---

* In *Śrī Caitanya-caritāmṛta,* Śrīla Prabhupāda translates *akṛta-droha* as humble.

is also a devotional sentiment. It is far superior to the blind enjoyer, who goes along merrily in ignorance. The humble devotee, as expressed by Bhaktivinoda Ṭhākura, captures the dictionary meaning of *humble*: "aware of one's shortcomings." But beyond the dictionary meaning, Bhaktivinoda Ṭhākura is seeing everything in its relation to Kṛṣṇa. Having reached the point of hopelessness, he thinks he cannot be saved; and yet, going beyond hopelessness, he receives the message Kṛṣṇa's pure devotee compassionately delivers to him. There is hope. Kṛṣṇa has saved so many fallen souls, and He can save another. *Śaraṇāgati,* therefore, teaches us that humility is not a superficial thing. It is deep, honest, and natural, and it comes when a conditioned soul sees his failure and unpretentiously begs Kṛṣṇa for forgiveness and engagement in devotional service.

In his *Bhagavad-gītā As It Is,* Śrīla Prabhupāda writes: "Humility means that one should not be anxious to have the satisfaction of being honored by others."

And Lord Caitanya in *Śikṣāṣṭaka* gives the ultimate expression of humility: "One should chant the holy name of the Lord in a humble state of mind, thinking oneself lower than the straw in the street; one should be more tolerant than a tree, devoid of all sense of false prestige, and ready to offer all respect to others. In such a state of mind one can chant the holy name of the Lord constantly."

Humility is glorious and is one of the prime qualities of a transcendentally situated person. Śrīla Prabhupāda says, "The qualities of humbleness and meekness lead very quickly to spiritual realization."

Out of humility the *sannyāsī* goes from door to door, not exactly to beg but to awaken the householders to Kṛṣṇa consciousness. Meeting many difficulties in his traveling and preaching, the *sannyāsī* remains tolerant and humble and therefore gains the strength to go on preaching.

No one is fit to approach Kṛṣṇa's lotus feet unless he is humble. Humility before Kṛṣṇa is natural, of course, because He is the Supreme. Similarly, humility before the Vaiṣṇava is also natural, because he is the servant of the greatest.

When Kṛṣṇadāsa Kavirāja said, "I am so sinful that if you simply remember my name you will lose all the credit for your pious activities," he actually meant it. Such humility, however, is not so cheap that one can obtain it simply by writing "Humbly yours" before signing his name. It cannot be imitated; it must develop gradually. If one sincerely desires to be a devotee and faces facts honestly, then he must drop all arrogance and pride. Following in the path of the previous *ācāryas,* he will note how Lord Caitanya showed humility by accepting Himself as a fool before His spiritual master, Īśvara Purī. An honest devotee will conclude, "What am I compared to Lord Caitanya? My place is humble. I have very stupidly entered the cycle of birth and death. So what do I have to be proud of?"

When Lord Caitanya came into the company of Māyāvādī *sannyāsīs* at Benares, He humbly sat by the place where everyone washed their feet. The Māyāvādī *sannyāsīs* had taken elevated seats, and when they saw Śrī Caitanya Mahāprabhu so humble and meek, they thought He must be lamenting. They couldn't understand His meekness. His humility was inconceivable.

Rūpa Gosvāmī and Haridāsa Ṭhākura also exemplified humility by living in a hut at a distance from the temple in Jagannātha Purī. And in recognition of their humility Lord Caitanya daily visited them, giving them His intimate blessings.

Sanātana Gosvāmī showed his humility in all his acts. Thinking himself impure and fearing that the temple *pūjārīs* might brush his body while walking on the road, Sanātana chose to walk on the beach instead. The price of such humility was that the hot sand burnt the soles of his feet. But the glory of his humility was that he didn't feel the burning and that Lord Caitanya embraced him as His dear devotee.

Sanātana Gosvāmī, in surrendering to Lord Caitanya, expresses the perfect humility of the disciple: "I was born in a low family, and my associates are all low-class men. I myself am fallen and am the lowest of men. Indeed, I have passed my whole life fallen in the well of sinful materialism. I do not know what is beneficial for me and what is detrimental. Nonetheless, in ordinary dealings people consider me a scholar, and I am also thinking of myself as such. Out of Your causeless mercy, You have delivered me from the materialistic path. Now, by the same causeless mercy, please tell me what my duty is." (Cc. *Madhya* 20.99–101)

His Divine Grace Śrīla Prabhupāda displayed the epitome of humility in coming to America. He had no prestige; he described himself as an "insignificant beggar." Undergoing constant difficulties and old age, living in a foreign land and a dangerous Kali-yuga city—the heart of a degradation no Vaiṣṇava *ācārya* had ever seen—Śrīla Prabhupāda was constantly humble. He preached to whomever would listen. And he tolerated insults, robbery, the madness of LSD-intoxicated hippies, the ignorance of the people, the constant proximity of meat-eaters and sex-mongers, and his own poverty and obscurity without becoming angry or discouraged. Gradually, Prabhupāda succeeded in gaining disciples and instilled in them faith in Kṛṣṇa consciousness. Years later, when the Kṛṣṇa consciousness movement was thriving all over the world, Śrīla Prabhupāda never took any credit for what he had done. He said he had done nothing at all except to faithfully carry out the orders of his spiritual master. He was, therefore, humble in taking the order of his spiritual master on his head, humble in coming to America, humble in enduring difficulties, and humble in his fabulous success.

Let us pray to be humble devotees and, taking the order of *guru* and Kṛṣṇa on our heads, carry out Their instructions: "Whomever you meet, tell them about Kṛṣṇa."

3

A devotee is truthful, *satya-sāra.*

To be truthful you first have to know the truth. Being truthful is not just a matter of refraining from telling lies. There is a legend that young George Washington was very truthful because he admitted, "I cannot tell a lie; it was I who cut down the cherry tree." But that is not *truthful.* Young George was candid in honestly admitting that he did a stupid thing. Real truthfulness, however, begins when one knows the Supreme Personality of Godhead, the Absolute Truth:

> Just try to learn the truth by approaching a spiritual master. Inquire from him submissively and render service unto him. The self-realized soul can impart knowledge unto you because he has seen the truth
>
> —Bg. 4.34

The Absolute Truth is Kṛṣṇa, as He is described in the first verse of *Śrīmad-Bhāgavatam:*

> O my Lord, Śrī Kṛṣṇa, son of Vasudeva, O all-pervading Personality of Godhead, I offer my respectful obeisances unto You. I meditate upon Lord Śrī Kṛṣṇa because He is the Absolute Truth and the primeval cause of all cause of the creation, sustenance and destruction of the manifested universes. He is

directly and indirectly conscious of all manifestations, and He is independent because there is no other cause beyond Him. It is He only who first imparted the Vedic knowledge unto the heart of Brahmājī, the original living being. By Him even the great sages and demigods are placed into illusion, as one is bewildered by the illusory representations of water seen in fire, or land seen on water. Only because of Him do the material universes, temporarily manifested by the reactions of the three modes of nature, appear factual, although they are unreal. I therefore meditate upon Him, Lord Śrī Kṛṣṇa, who is eternally existent in the transcendental abode, which is forever free from the illusory representations of the material world. I meditate upon Him, for He is the Absolute Truth.

—*Bhāg*. 1.1.1

One can study this verse for his entire lifetime to appreciate how Kṛṣṇa is the Absolute Truth. In his Introduction to *Śrīmad-Bhāgavatam*, Śrīla Prabhupāda takes the phrase *paraṁ satyam* from this verse and translates it "the Absolute Truth." He then defines *paraṁ satyaṁ* as "the ultimate source of all energies." In other words, the Absolute Truth is the cause of all causes, and *Śrīmad-Bhāgavatam*, in the first verse, has hit the target of the Absolute Truth by defining Him in His personal feature as the Supreme God. God is a personal term to describe the controller. There are many gods, or controllers, but when we speak of the Supreme Godhead, then we mean Kṛṣṇa, the cause of all causes.

So the Absolute Truth as the Supreme Person, Śrī Kṛṣṇa, is revealed in *Śrīmad-Bhāgavatam's* opening verse. In fact, the entire Vedic literature is proclaiming Kṛṣṇa as the Absolute Truth. This is also stated in *Bhagavad-gītā* [10.8], *ahaṁ sarvasya prabhavaḥ*—the Absolute Truth is that from which everything else emanates. Since there are countless living beings coming from the Absolute Truth, the Absolute Truth must also contain personality. Elsewhere in *Śrīmad-Bhāgavatam,* the author, Śrīla Vyāsadeva, describes that the highest feature of the Absolute Truth is Bhagavān, the Supreme Person.

Atheistic philosophers deny Kṛṣṇa as the Absolute Truth and even deny Him as a historical person. They also deny the existence of the spirit soul and reject the concept of a personal God. Yet despite their evolutionary theories, speculations about life coming from chemicals, and wild theories about creation, they are unable to explain the origin of existence. The question vital for every human being—"What is the meaning of existence? Where have I come from? What is the mission of life beyond animal survival? What is after death?"—cannot be reduced to chemical and biological theories. The answers to these questions lie in the realm of philosophy. But philosophy without religion is dry speculation, whereas religion without philosophy is merely sentiment. *Śrīmad-Bhāgavatam's* presentation of Lord Kṛṣṇa as the Supreme Truth, however, satisfies the criteria of both perfect philosophy and perfect religion. The perfect philosophy is *Vedānta,* wherein the cause of all causes is explained with logic and reasoning, and the perfect religious practice is *bhakti-yoga,* or devotional service to the Supreme Lord.

Persons seeking the Absolute Truth, who are dissatisfied with material sense gratification and mental speculation, must approach the genuine authorities in disciplic succession. Even if a person wants to learn a mundane skill, he has to learn from authorities. In the philosophic search for truth there are many contesting philosophers, all speculating on the mental level. But the only possible way to reach transcendence is the path of the *ācāryas*, the recognized saintly philosophers who have themselves realized the Absolute Truth through the process of disciplic succession. The words of Vedic authorities like Śukadeva Gosvāmī, Śrīla Vyāsadeva, and others, and the evidence of their personal spiritual attainment, are sufficient to convince a sincere inquirer.

Once we recognize that Kṛṣṇa is the Absolute Truth, there is an obligation to distribute this truth *widely* and thus combat falsity. Most people blindly try to deny the fact that everything in this universe is owned and controlled by the Supreme Lord. Only if civilized humanity recognizes the proprietorship of God can there be peace and prosperity in the world. For want of this most basic knowledge of the Supreme Personality of Godhead as the proprietor, men violate the laws of God and nature, incurring great karmic suffering.

Knowledge of the truth makes us free. The concept of the body as the self is false, as anyone who witnesses the death of a dear one can testify. We see our friend, relative or pet is gone, and yet the body remains. The body, therefore, is not the self but the vehicle that carries the self, just as a car carries the driver. The real self is the eternal spirit soul. Life in the material world, suffering the changes of birth, death, disease, and old age, is not the true, constitutional situation of the self. We are meant for the eternal, spiritual world. The spiritual world is true, and only due to a false notion of the self (false ego) are the living entities imprisoned in the material world birth after birth. Distribution of the knowledge of Kṛṣṇa consciousness is meant to free the soul from his bondage to material life.

But what about young George Washington? Doesn't being truthful also mean "telling the truth", being very honest? Yes. There is a story in the *Upaniṣads* praising this quality. A boy approached Gautama Muni for instruction. The system was that the *guru* would only accept the son of a *brāhmaṇa* as his student. When Gautama Muni asked the boy who his father was, the boy didn't know. He went to ask his mother. But his mother, a promiscuous maidservant, had had so many men that she couldn't say for certain who the boy's father was. The boy returned to Gautama Muni and guilelessly reported that he didn't know who his father was. Seeing this boy's complete honesty, the *guru* said, "You are actually a *brāhmaṇa* because of your honesty," and he accepted the boy as his disciple. Actually, a *brāhmaṇa* is so honest that if a thief asks him, "Where is your money?" he will not lie.

And yet, ultimately, honesty leads us again to our definition of truth: Kṛṣṇa. I may not know my earthly father, but in transcendental reality, Kṛṣṇa is my father. To say that Kṛṣṇa is my father is not a facetious lie but is the Absolute Truth. So if a thief asks for my money and I say I've given it to Kṛṣṇa, that is also true. In complete truthfulness, I am not required to turn Kṛṣṇa's money over to the thief. But I should never hide anything to protect my own interests. If Kṛṣṇa wants me to protect His interests, then I must be true to that ultimate obligation. Kṛṣṇa asked Yudhiṣṭhira to tell a lie during the Battle of Kurukṣetra, but Yudhiṣṭhira hesitated. Some commentators falsely cite his lying as the cause of Yudhiṣṭhira's having to see hell. But actually Yudhiṣṭhira's only fault was his hesitation to carry out Kṛṣṇa's order to tell a lie. Truthfulness, therefore, is doing whatever Kṛṣṇa desires.

Of the four principles of religion—austerity, cleanliness, mercifulness, and truthfulness—only truthfulness remains in Kali-yuga. When Mahārāja Parīkṣit found the bull of religion after it had been attacked by the personified Kali, only one of the bull's legs, that representing truthfulness, remained. This means that although people are living sinful, hedonistic lives, still in this age a willingness to hear about Kṛṣṇa remains. When Śrīla Prabhupāda came to America, he found more or less everyone engaged in sinful activities; but when he exposed these activities as sinful, and when he revealed the truth of Kṛṣṇa, the hedonists reformed.

Those devotees following Prabhupāda should be very truthful, like real *brāhmaṇas.* This certainly means in their own behavior they should not cheat. The first truthfulness of a disciple is to keep his promise to avoid sinful acts and always chant sixteen rounds of *japa* on his beads. Nor should a devotee engage in illegal activities. Although Kṛṣṇa consciousness is transcendental to mundane law, that mundane law is rarely to be violated. And even an ordinary person can appreciate such truthfulness. Society must recognize the members of the Kṛṣṇa consciousness movement as religious persons. But we must be truthful in the ultimate sense, acting not for our own interests but for Kṛṣṇa's interests. However, we must first understand who is Kṛṣṇa. He is the Supreme Truth, and—*satyaṁ paraṁ dhīmahi*—we have to meditate on the Supreme Truth by chanting Hare Kṛṣṇa. Then we can render pure devotional service and be effective in our distribution of the Absolute Truth, which can alone save mankind in this disastrous age.

4

A devotee is equal to everyone, *sama*.

vidyā-vinaya-sampanne
brāhmaṇe gavi hastini
śuni caiva śva-pāke ca
paṇḍitāḥ sama-darśinaḥ

The humble sages, by virtue of true knowledge, see with equal vision a learned and gentle brāhmaṇa, a cow, an elephant, a dog and a dog-eater [outcaste].

—Bg. 5.18

We are each a tiny spirit soul, in measurement one ten-thousandth the tip of a hair. This understanding is the basis of equal vision. Neither a bodily sentiment nor a concocted philosophy proclaiming everyone as God, equal vision is the transcendental fact: all species of life are actually infinitesimal spirit souls covered by different, external shapes. Many different-size trucks and cars may be on the highway, but the driver of each is a human being. Similarly, within each body in all species on all planets of the material world is the infinitesimal, eternal spirit soul. Each spirit soul has taken residence in a particular body because of his *karma*.

puruṣaḥ prakṛti-stho hi
bhuṅkte prakṛti-jān guṇān
kāraṇaṁ guṇa-saṅgo 'sya
sad-asad-yoni-janmasu

> The living entity in material nature thus follows the ways of life, enjoying the three modes of nature. This is due to his association with that material nature. Thus he meets with good and evil amongst various species.
> —Bg. 13.22

Kṛṣṇa also declares that all the living entities, or *jīvas*, are His "eternally fragmented parts and parcels." They have come into this material world due to their desires and are now struggling with the senses and the mind.

The devotee sees all creatures from this perspective of knowledge. Wherever he sees a living creature displaying the six symptoms of life, namely birth, growth, duration, producing by-products, dwindling, and death, he knows a spirit soul inhabits that form, whether a human being, an animal, an insect, a bird, or a plant.

In addition to perceiving the presence of the individual soul, the learned devotee knows the Supreme Soul is also there within the heart of every living entity. Therefore, in *Bhagavad-gītā* 15.15 Kṛṣṇa declares, "I am seated in everyone's heart, and from Me comes remembrance, knowledge and forgetfulness." He reaffirms, "The Supreme Lord is situated in everyone's heart, O Arjuna, and is directing the wanderings of all living entities, who are seated on a machine made of material energy." (Bg. 18.61) A devotee acts, therefore, on the basis of this knowledge of the soul and the Supersoul. We have heard of the popular philosophy, "a reverence for all life." The philosophy of Kṛṣṇa consciousness supplies us with the scientific basis for such a nonviolent attitude toward all living beings. One should not unnecessarily take the life of another creature, because in essence the lowly creature is equal to the more elevated creature. All are spirit souls undergoing different periods of *karma*. If even the lowly insect is a spirit soul not to be killed at a man's whim, how much more so valuable animals like the cow should be protected and not killed.

Seeing with equal vision, however, does not mean that we treat each person exactly the same. But our intention should be the same: to share Kṛṣṇa consciousness with one and all. Lord Caitanya was able to engage even the jungle tigers, lions, and elephants in chanting Hare Kṛṣṇa. This is not possible for us, but nevertheless, we can relate in a Kṛṣṇa conscious way even to the animals. At least we need not kill them simply for our sense gratification. Especially we can approach the human beings—always seeing them as eternal servants of the Lord and relating to them in Kṛṣṇa consciousness.

In *The Nectar of Devotion,* Rūpa Gosvāmī tells us how to relate to the Supreme Lord, the devotee, the innocent persons, and the demon. Each case is a matter of reciprocating in Kṛṣṇa consciousness. We should worship and serve the Supreme Lord, the object of all devotional service. With the devotee we should be friends. With the innocent nondevotee we should use all facility to give him the gift of Kṛṣṇa consciousness. And with the devout atheist we should leave him to him own devices, to be dealt with by Kṛṣṇa according to the law of *karma.* Sometimes, however, the dedicated and empowered devotees reach even the stone-like hearts of the avowed atheists through distribution of the Lord's mercy as *prasādam, kīrtana,* and Kṛṣṇa conscious literature.

In the case of the *mahā-bhāgavata,* or first-class devotee, the distinctions between demon and devotee disappear; he sees everyone as the eternal servant of Kṛṣṇa. He sees that nothing is beyond the Lord's control and that even the demons are playing a part in His complete plan. The *mahā-bhāgavata* is merged in meditation of the

Lord and sees, therefore, everything within the Lord's creation as spiritual. But to do practical missionary work on behalf of the Supreme Lord, the *mahā-bhāgavata* sometimes comes down to assume the role of a preacher. At that time, for preaching, he sees distinctions between devotee and nondevotee, for the purpose of advancing Kṛṣṇa's cause in the material world.

As the devotee is equal to all, so is the Supreme Lord. The demons, citing how Lord Kṛṣṇa repeatedly takes the side of the demigod Indra against the *asuras,* once accused the Lord of favoring the demigods. But Śukadeva Gosvāmī explains that Lord Viṣṇu is actually impartial. He offers to one and all, if they surrender to Him, freedom from the reactions of *karma.* Those who reject Him entangle themselves in their own actions and reactions under the influence of the time factor. The Lord is not to blame. Kṛṣṇa's actions are free from all material duality. Whether His actions appear as enmity or blessings, whatever He does is good. It is up to the living entity, therefore, to understand the all-good intentions of Kṛṣṇa and to properly receive His blessings.

tat te 'nukampāṁ susamīkṣamāṇo
bhuñjāna evātma-kṛtaṁ vipākam
hṛd-vāg-vapurbhir vidadham namas te
jīveta yo mukti-pade sa dāya-bhāk

My dear Lord, one who earnestly waits for You to bestow Your causeless mercy upon him, all the while patiently suffering the reactions of his past misdeeds and offering You respectful obeisances with his heart, words and body, is surely eligible for liberation, for it has become his rightful claim.

—*Bhāg.* 10.14.8

This is the natural tendency of a devotee—that he is always inclined to the Supreme Lord. And Kṛṣṇa, although inclined toward everyone, becomes especially inclined toward His devotee.

samo 'ham sarva-bhūteṣu
na me dveṣyo 'sti na priyaḥ
te bhajanti tu mām bhaktyā
mayi te teṣu cāpy aham

I envy no one, nor am I partial to anyone. I am equal to all. But whoever renders service unto Me in devotion is a friend, is in Me, and I am also a friend to him.

—Bg. 9.29

In the history of Prahlāda Mahārāja, we have a clear example of the devotee's equality to all. Prahlāda's asuric teacher tried to instruct him in the science of diplomacy—how to rule and divide, how to make friends and subdue enemies. But Prahlāda Mahārāja replied that this teaching that distinguishes "my friend" from "my enemy" is a creation of the external energy (*māyā*) of the Supreme. Prahlāda Mahārāja said:

When the Supreme Personality of Godhead is pleased with the living entity because of his devotional service, one becomes a *paṇḍita* and does not make distinctions between enemies, friends and himself. Intelligently, he then thinks, 'Every one of us is an eternal servant of God, and therefore we are not different from one another.'

—*Bhāg*. 7.5.12

This equipoised attitude is based on the philosophy of oneness of all souls. The *Īśopaniṣad* proclaims *ekatvam anupaśyataḥ:* a learned man should see all people alike, regardless of their community, race or nation, because of the presence of the Supreme Lord in each person's heart.

The quality of being equal to everyone is realized among the servants of the Lord. Śrīla Prabhupāda wrote in one purport:

> Everyone should be friendly for the service of the Lord. Everyone should praise another's service to the Lord and not be proud of his own service. This is the way of Vaiṣṇava thinking, Vaikuṇṭha thinking. There may be rivalries and apparent competitions between servants in performing service, but in the Vaikuṇṭha planets the service of another servant is appreciated, not condemned. This is Vaikuṇṭha competition. There is no question of enmity between servants. Everyone should be allowed to render service to the Lord to the best of his ability, and everyone should appreciate the service of others. Such are the activities of Vaikuṇṭha. Since everyone is a servant, everyone is on the same platform and is allowed to serve the Lord according to his ability.
>
> —*Bhāg*. 7.5.12, purport

5

A devotee is faultless, *nidoṣa.*

How could anyone claim to be without fault? But a devotee who is surrendered in body, mind, and words to Kṛṣṇa is always executing Kṛṣṇa's will and repeating Kṛṣṇa's message; therefore, as Kṛṣṇa, the Supreme Perfect, is faultless, so His fully surrendered devotee is faultless. Those things that appear as faults in the devotee do not mar his faultlessness. Śrīla Prabhupāda explains in *The Nectar of Devotion*:

> The example is given that on the full moon there are some spots which may appear to be pockmarks. Still, the illumination spread by the full moon cannot be checked. Similarly, a little fault in the midst of volumes of devotional service is not at all to be counted as fault. Attachment for Kṛṣṇa is transcendental bliss. Amid unlimited volumes of transcendental bliss, a spot of some material defect cannot act in any way.

Even if a devotee accidentally deviates from pure devotional activities, he should still be considered saintly. The *Nṛsiṁha Purāṇa* states: "If a person has completely engaged his mind, body, and activities in the service of the Supreme Godhead, but externally he is found to be engaged in some abominable activities, these abominable activities will surely be very quickly vanquished by the influence of his staunch devotional force."

The *rightness* and purity of the devotee's resolve to serve Kṛṣṇa is so great that it rectifies all faults. But to see this, one requires devotional vision. The nondevotee will see faults even in the greatest devotee, whereas the devotee will always see Kṛṣṇa's pure devotee as faultless. In his *Śaraṇāgati*, Bhaktivinoda Ṭhākura prays to always has this devotional vision:

> Mud and foam are seen in the waters of the Ganges; that is the inherent nature of river water. Yet Ganges water never loses its transcendental nature.
>
> One may likewise find defects in the body of a Vaiṣṇava, yet his body is always spiritual, never material. That person who criticizes the body of a Vaiṣṇava falls into deadly irreligion.
>
> —*Śaraṇāgati, Bhajana-lālasā* 6.1–2

The "faults," then, are only the imagination of persons with material vision. If the devotee mispronounces a Sanskrit verse, technically speaking we can say he has committed an error, but that error doesn't undermine his faultless position—that he is trying to glorify Kṛṣṇa under the order of the spiritual master. The First Canto of *Śrīmad-Bhāgavatam* explains:

> That literature which is full of descriptions of the transcendental glories of the name, fame, forms, pastimes, etc., of the unlimited Supreme Lord is a different creation, full of transcendental words directed toward bringing about a revolution in the impious lives of this world's misdirected civilization. Such transcendental literatures, even though imperfectly composed, are heard, sung, and accepted by purified men who are thoroughly honest.
>
> —*Bhāg*. 1.5.11

Śrīla Prabhupāda's first edition of *Śrīmad-Bhāgavatam* came out in India under difficult conditions and contained grammatical, spelling, and printing errors. But the philosophy was completely perfect and in *paramparā* from Lord Caitanya and Lord Kṛṣṇa; therefore, those who are "thoroughly honest" have no difficulty overlooking the errors. Śrīla Prabhupāda and his disciples were very happy in subsequent years when they came out with a new edition of the same volume with technical errors removed, but they never thought that the original volume lacked any transcendental perfection. Rather, those volumes are treasured today as collector's items and are read with as much pleasure and gain as the technically improved volumes. The very errors remind us how Śrīla Prabhupāda first published these books, without any income or assistance, overseeing all aspects of the production, personally collecting the funds, proofreading, and transporting the paper to the printer. The devotees see the technical mistakes as the mud in the Ganges, which doesn't affect the purifying effect of the holy Ganges; and they see Śrīla Prabhupāda's own humble statement about the matter as confirmation of the true nature of faultlessness:

> We are sure, therefore, that everyone in the human society will welcome *Śrīmad-Bhāgavatam,* even though it is now presented with so many faults, for it is recommended by Śrī Nārada, who has very kindly appeared in this chapter.
>
> —*Bhāg.* 1.5.11, purport

So the quality of faultlessness manifests when a devotee is fully engaged in the service of Kṛṣṇa. The true identity of a living entity is to be a servitor of the

Supreme Lord. When this realization is mature, the devotee goes to join Kṛṣṇa in his liberated, eternal, spiritual body. Even while in the material world, however, he is liberated by being fully situated in the service of the Supreme Lord. We must determine whether a person is faultless by his activities in devotional service, not by other symptoms. As long as he is in the material world, there will be material necessities, illness, imperfection of senses, and various perceivable limitations and defects; but these do not constitute faults. The devotee is saintly, because he has right resolved to serve Kṛṣṇa and *guru*.

It is possible for a rascal to masquerade as a faultless pure devotee, to try to show himself as an advanced spiritual leader, and to cheat people for his own profit. But an intelligent devotee can detect such a fraud. A pure-hearted devotee, or someone sincerely following his orders, will not act to harm or abuse anyone. Despite the presence of rascals, we should go ahead wholeheartedly honoring and following the instructions of the pure devotee. In the guise of holy men and devotees, imposters have come, but that does not mean there is no real devotee. The real devotee is known by his acts strictly in accordance with *paramparā*. He will never abuse the honor, service, or money he receives on behalf of Kṛṣṇa; we can trust him with our life. He will do good for all humanity, because he will live and preach the message of Kṛṣṇa.

6

A devotee is magnanimous, vadānya.

The dictionary defines *magnanimous* as "Noble of mind and spirit; generous in forgiving; above revenge or resentment; unselfish, gracious . . . from Latin, *magnanimous,* 'great souled.'"

Rūpa Gosvāmī, in his prayer to Lord Caitanya, gives a brilliant expression of the magnanimity of the devotee:

namo mahā-vadānyāya kṛṣṇa-prema-pradāya te
kṛṣṇaya kṛṣṇa-caitanya-nāmne gaura-tviṣe namaḥ

> O most munificent incarnation! You are Kṛṣṇa Himself appearing as Śrī Kṛṣṇa Caitanya Mahāprabhu. You have assumed the golden color of Śrīmatī Rādhārāṇī, and You are widely distributing pure love of Kṛṣṇa. We offer our respectful obeisances unto You.
>
> —Cc. *Madhya* 19.53

According to this prayer, Lord Caitanya is the most magnanimous of all benefactors because He is distributing the gift of love of God, which is infinitely superior to all other gifts.

Everyone can agree that a more enduring benefit surpasses a temporary one. An example of temporary assistance would be to find a lost child, take him in, give him a meal and rest, and then release him again—lost. But to take the lost child to his wealthy, loving parents is a greater benefit. So he who grants us eternal benefit is like the person who returns the lost child to his original, happy home.

Life in the material world is full of suffering, and one who tries to help but is ineffectual is sometimes derisively called a "do-gooder." Ultimately, his attempt to help others becomes meddling; he cannot do good. Why? Because people are *meant* to suffer due to their own sinful reactions. Life in this material world is like life in a state prison. Although reforms can be made in the standard of prison life, a reformer is not allowed to make the prison a free, happy place. One purpose of the prison is to restrict the normal, free movements of its inmates. Similarly, this material world is designed to give trouble to all who come here under the laws of birth, death, disease, and old age.

Or take the example of a hospital. A patient may be on a very strict diet, but if a do-gooder gives the patient highly spiced, fried foods and rich deserts, the patient may become deathly ill or the meddler thrown out of the hospital. The do-gooder did not know that the patient's fasting was meant for curing him.

In this material world everyone is acting under the force of their *karma,* and no one can change it, try as he might. Suffering and happiness are destined for every living being. The do-gooders cannot understand the laws of nature, and they try in different concocted ways to evade the strict laws of material nature. Yet their efforts are always baffled, and they can never be effective, magnanimous persons. They may want to do good, but they don't know how. If a do-gooder dives into a river, swims out to save a drowning man, but returns only with the man's shirt, leaving the man in the river to drown, everyone will consider such a rescuer a useless fool. Similarly, the real person within each of us, the eternal soul, can never be saved by welfare attempts that only tend to the "shirt" of the material body, which is covering the self.

Eternal benefit can only be granted through the process of *bhakti,* or the activities of loving service to Kṛṣṇa. Impersonal eternality cannot help any more than the benefits of temporary material happiness. Lord Kṛṣṇa tell Arjuna in the B*hagavad-gītā* 2.12, "Never was there a time when I did not exist, nor you, nor all these kings; nor in the future shall any of us cease to be." This proves that our individuality is never lost; after death we take another material body. Or if we are to enter eternal life, we also do so in our eternal individuality, as pure servants of the Personality of Godhead. The conception of an eternally liberated state where there is no individuality, no individual soul, and no Supreme Personality of Godhead is a hellish concoction by speculative Māyāvādī philosophers and is not supported by direct Vedic *śāstra.*

The truly magnanimous welfare worker must, therefore, transcend material meddling as well as concocted doctrines of eternality in an impersonal, godless condition. He must teach pure love of God. The eternal, individual soul's relationship of loving service to the Supreme Godhead is the universal principle in all religions. There are religious designations such as Christian, Moslem, or Hindu, but love of God is the essence, just as, for example, different styles of eating exist in India, America, and China, but the essence is the same—satisfaction of the palate, relief of hunger, and nutrition. But one may argue, "Yes, but my religion is the best."

"The best religion?" The test is given in the *Śrīmad-Bhāgavatam*: That religion is best which produces in its follower's *symptoms* of pure love of God.

According to *Śrīmad-Bhāgavatam,* pure love of God must be prosecuted without interruption or motivation; that alone will completely satisfy the self. Love of God is not the possession of a particular religious sect, but may be found wherever there are the symptoms of unmotivated, uninterrupted service to God. When pure love of God is operating, the devotee is not serving the Lord with a motive that God should give him "his daily bread;" or that in return for his worship God should send him to a heavenly planet. The pure devotee is motivated purely by the desire to please the Supreme Person, to whom he has become spontaneously attracted in ecstatic love.

The name Kṛṣṇa describes the Supreme Person as "all attractive." Therefore, when a devotee begins to realize God's all-attractive name, fame, form, and activities, he gives up all other consideration for gain or safety and simply dedicates himself to serving the All-Attractive Person. Dhruva Mahārāja was performing austerities to see God for obtaining a material boon; this is known as approaching God as the supreme order supplier. But when Dhruva saw the all-beautiful Supreme Person, he relinquished all other desires but that of surrendering himself to Kṛṣṇa. Dhruva Mahārāja said, "Now that I have seen You, I am completely satisfied."

When a devotee wants only to serve the Supreme Person, then he is qualified to go to the eternal, spiritual world. This pure teaching of love of God is the essence of the teaching of Christ, Kṛṣṇa, or Mohammed. The apparent differences or contradictions in the religious doctrines in various parts of the world have arisen because of the inability of the followers to relinquish their material compromises and accept the heart of all religious instructions: *surrender to God.* The eternal teaching of Godhead cannot be changed and are always open to those who seek the ultimate truth. Kṛṣṇa has clearly stated in *Bhagavad-gītā* that there is no other way to reach Him except by *bhakti,* pure devotional service.

bhaktya mām abhijānāti
yāvān yaś cāsmi tattvataḥ
tato māṁ tattvato jñātvā
viśate tad-anantaram

> One can understand Me as I am, as the Supreme Personality of Godhead, only by devotional service. And when one is in full consciousness of Me by such devotion, he can enter into the kingdom of God.
>
> —Bg. 18.55

Lord Kṛṣṇa has positively concluded the *Bhagavad-gītā* 18.66 with the order, "Abandon all varieties of religion and just surrender unto Me. I shall deliver you from all sinful reactions. Do not fear." But because an ordinary man, even if he believes in God, may find it difficult to follow Kṛṣṇa's pure teachings and surrender everything to Him, Lord Caitanya came only five hundred years ago and taught a sublime and easy method of surrender to Kṛṣṇa.

The Vedic literature reveals Lord Caitanya as Lord Kṛṣṇa Himself. But in His appearance as Lord Caitanya, He acted not as God but as the pure devotee of God. He took the position of the greatest, most loving of all of the Lord's devotees, Śrīmatī Rādhārāṇī, and thus showed the world how a pure devotee should love God with all his mind, words, and activities. His demonstration of devotional service, therefore, is most authoritative.

Lord Caitanya freely gave the gift of love of God unconditionally. Before Lord Caitanya's appearance, no religious teacher had taught that a devotee may love the Supreme Being with all the personal feeling and fervor that a lover offers to his beloved. Lord Caitanya, however, taught that what exists in this material world as the most intense relationship—the love between man and woman—is in fact a perverted reflection of the original, spiritual relationship between God and His parts and parcels. This is not easily understood and is generally misunderstood by anyone who approaches it with a material, or sexual conception. It is the highest understanding of love of God.

Prior to Lord Caitanya, God was seen somewhat impersonally or at best as the Father, the Provider. But Lord Caitanya taught that a devotee may worship God in different *rasas,* known as "mellows." The Supreme Person can be approached as the supreme unknown, as the supreme master, as the supreme friend, the supreme child, and the supreme lover. In this way, a devotee can dedicate all his life's activities in devotional service to his supreme loveable object—Kṛṣṇa, the Supreme Personality of Godhead. And Kṛṣṇa, being the reservoir of all pleasures and *rasas,* can reciprocate with each devotee according to his devotional inclination. One can understand this science of *rasa* only by taking guidance from a spiritual master in disciplic succession, from one who understands love of God according to the authorized directions of *guru, śāstra,* and *sādhu.*

Lord Caitanya did not introduce this science of love of God as a new thing; it exists eternally as the original relationship of all living beings with the Supreme, and it is described in Vedic literatures. Lord Caitanya's unique contribution was to distribute the mellows of pure love of God in a very simple method.

Lord Caitanya appeared in Kali-yuga, the age that began five thousand years ago and that will continue for another 432,000 years. As there are material seasons, some harsh, like winter, and some mild, like spring, so Kali-yuga is the harshest, most godless of all the millennia. *Śrīmad-Bhāgavatam* describes the people in this age as very unfortunate, very slow in the matter of self-realization, and usually cheated. Lord Caitanya was most magnanimous, therefore, in giving the fallen souls of this age an easy process to attain the highest standard of love of God. Even in former millennia when conditions were more conducive for spiritual life, the full mercy of Lord Caitanya's *saṅkīrtana* movement was not present in the proportion that it is now for the fallen souls of Kali-yuga.

Why did Lord Caitanya do this? It is His inconceivable mercy. He is the most magnanimous person, and this is His gift. Others—prophets, sons, and servants of God—gave mostly moral instructions for religious behavior. Even Kṛṣṇa Himself did not reveal the secret of loving surrender to Him. Only when appearing in the form of Lord Caitanya did He give the most magnanimous gift. Therefore, when we want to speak of the quality of magnanimity, we must put forward the example of Lord Caitanya. He showed all the qualities of a devotee and especially the quality of magnanimity.

Lord Caitanya's method of loving surrender to God was the chanting of Hare Kṛṣṇa. Lord Caitanya taught that in the holy name of Kṛṣṇa, Kṛṣṇa Himself appears. One can, therefore, attain full love of God simply by chanting His holy name. Lord Caitanya also taught that for full effect the chanter of the holy name should lead a holy life and chant without offense. Lord Caitanya saved two great sinners of His time, Jagāi and Mādhāi, demonstrating that even the greatest rogues could be saved. But after forgiving and blessing them, He instructed them to lead a saintly life.

Lord Caitanya stressed five methods of devotional service: (1) to chant Hare Kṛṣṇa, (2) to live in a holy place, (3) to read *Bhagavad-gītā* and *Śrīmad-Bhāgavatam,* (4) to worship the Deity of Kṛṣṇa, and (5) to associate with devotees. This process of chanting Hare Kṛṣṇa and living in Kṛṣṇa consciousness was the magnanimous gift of Kṛṣṇa in His most merciful form of Lord Caitanya. He instructed His followers to write books and propagate His method so that it would be followed by people of the future.

One great contemporary follower of Lord Caitanya was the famous philosopher and logician Sārvabhauma Bhaṭṭācārya. Sārvabhauma Bhaṭṭācārya composed a prayer of appreciation for Lord Caitanya which describes His magnanimous gift to mankind:

vairāgya-vidyā-nija-bhakti-yoga-
śikṣārtham ekaḥ puruṣaḥ purāṇaḥ
śrī-kṛṣṇa-caitanya-śarīra-dhārī
kṛpāmbudhir yas tam ahaṁ prapadye

Let me take shelter of the Supreme Personality of Godhead, Śrī Kṛṣṇa, who has descended in the form of Lord Caitanya Mahāprabhu to teach us real knowledge, His devotional service and detachment from whatever does not foster Kṛṣṇa consciousness. He has descended because He is an ocean of transcendental mercy. Let me surrender unto His lotus feet.

—Cc. *Madhya* 6.254

Two of the essential features of this verse are that Lord Caitanya is described as teaching knowledge of renunciation and the science of surrender. All the great spiritual teachers have instructed that we should give up this material world and that our true home is in the eternal kingdom of God. Lord Caitanya's method of *vairāgya,* or renunciation, is especially easy for people in this fallen age. He said take *prasādam,* chant Hare Kṛṣṇa, and dance in ecstasy.

This same program, as demonstrated and taught all over India five hundred years ago by Lord Caitanya, came to America in 1965 and then spread worldwide by the mercy of His Divine Grace A. C. Bhaktivedanta Swami Prabhupāda. Śrīla Prabhupāda formed the International Society for Kṛṣṇa Consciousness (ISKCON) as the means of spreading the teachings of Lord Caitanya. And he published Lord Caitanya's instructions in many volumes of authorized books.

The brilliance of Śrīla Prabhupāda was his full faith in the order of his spiritual master and Lord Caitanya and his own distribution of their teachings without change. People thought Prabhupāda would never succeed, especially since he had come to the West so late in life and had no support. But Prabhupāda knew the real criteria of welfare work. He knew that nothing else he could do would be of any help, even if it gained him fame or following. Śrīla Prabhupāda was, therefore, prepared to give out pure Kṛṣṇa consciousness, even if only one or two listened. But because he was pure and empowered by Kṛṣṇa and because devotional service is the natural function of the soul, many persons took to his offering of Kṛṣṇa consciousness. And so the Kṛṣṇa consciousness movement is growing still and will continue to grow throughout the Kali-yuga.

This is the magnanimous gift of the holy life in Kali-yuga. By chanting Hare Kṛṣṇa even the most fallen persons, the millions and millions of Jagāis and Mādhāis all over the world in the different nations and races, can practice the path of surrender and renunciation as instructed by Lord Caitanya. They don't have to practice renunciation separately or with great austerity, but renunciation comes automatically through attaining the higher taste of devotional service.

vāsudeve bhagavati
bhakti-yogaḥ prayojitaḥ
janayaty āśu vairāgyam
jñānam ca yad ahaitukam

> By rendering devotional service unto the Personality of Godhead, Śrī Kṛṣṇa, one immediately acquires causeless knowledge and detachment from the world.
>
> —*Bhāg*. 1.2.7

Sārvabhauma Bhaṭṭācārya says that Lord Caitanya also taught us the science of surrender. The followers of Lord Caitanya have enunciated six symptoms of surrender: (1) to do everything favorable for the service of Kṛṣṇa, (2) to avoid everything unfavorable for Kṛṣṇa consciousness, (3) to have faith that only Kṛṣṇa is one's maintainer, (4) to believe that Kṛṣṇa is one's protector, (5) to realize that nothing takes place except by Kṛṣṇa's sanction, and (6) to feel oneself as fallen and therefore in need of Kṛṣṇa's mercy.

Without endeavoring for anything else, one should merge all his desires into the service of Kṛṣṇa by the standard practices of devotional service, beginning with hearing and chanting, under the guidance of an expert spiritual master. The science of surrender is a blissful process, and as a result, the devotee becomes a lover of Kṛṣṇa. The givers of this devotional process are indeed magnanimous.

Because we are living in the material world, a world of difficulty, a world governed by the forces of illusion and evil, there are always difficulties in distributing the magnanimous gifts of Lord Caitanya. But the devotees' desire to distribute Lord Caitanya's gifts, whatever the difficulties, is another indication of the nature of their magnanimity. As in the dictionary definition of *magnanimous*, they have neither resentment nor selfishness. The devotees distribute Kṛṣṇa consciousness freely, not for some reward but because they want to benefit others. They become unhappy, in fact, seeing others' suffering.

Lord Caitanya described Himself as a gardener who has harvested an overabundance of fruits. The fruits are compared to love of God, and Lord Caitanya, as the gardener, is also the distributor of the fruits. In *Śrī Caitanya-caritāmṛta* Kṛṣṇadāsa Kavirāja writes:

> Not considering who asked for it and who did not, nor who was fit and who unfit to receive it, Caitanya Mahāprabhu distributed the fruit of devotional service.
>
> The transcendental gardener, Śrī Caitanya Mahāprabhu, distributed handful after handful of fruit in all directions, and when the poor, hungry people ate the fruit, the gardener smiled with great pleasure.
>
> —Cc. *Ādi* 9.29–30

This is the vigorous, living purport of the quality of magnanimity. Lord Caitanya and His followers know that love of God is the greatest of all things, and they go on distributing it without self-motivation, without disappointment, and without being checked. Their magnanimity knows no bounds, and the good fortune of those who receive their gifts is unparalleled.

7

A devotee is mild, *mṛdu.*

> Because of the appearance of the autumn season, the water of the ocean becomes calm and quiet, just as a person developed in self-realization becomes free from disturbances by the three modes of material nature.
>
> —*Kṛṣṇa,* Vol. 1, Ch. 20, "Description of Autumn"

The ordinary man, because his mind and senses are agitated, is not calm and peaceful. His senses are madly and vainly engaged in pursuing happiness by eating, mating, sleeping, and defending; or he is hankering to engage in such acts; or he is lamenting at having futilely attempted to find happiness in the pleasures of the senses and the mind.

> While contemplating the objects of the senses, a person develops attachment for them, and from such attachment lust develops, and from lust anger arises. From anger, complete delusion arises, and from delusion bewilderment of memory. When memory is bewildered, intelligence is lost and when intelligence is lost, one falls down again into the material pool.
>
> —Bg. 2.62–63

The devotee avoids this chase after illusory material pleasure and its resultant suffering. He remains peaceful because he is satisfied in Kṛṣṇa consciousness. A man who already has a million dollars does not become frantic trying to obtain or enjoy the pleasures of a thousand dollars. The law-abiding citizen does not become feverish and panic-stricken at the appearance of the police force. Similarly, the transcendentalist, who is satisfied in realizing himself as the eternal servitor of the Supreme Lord, is neither wooed by the pleasures of the world nor shaken by adversities. His temperament is mild because he has nothing to gain and no one can deprive him of his Kṛṣṇa consciousness.

Explaining *yoga-samādhi* in Chapter Six of *Bhagavad-gītā,* Lord Kṛṣṇa uses the metaphor of a lamp in a windless place to describe the constant, undisturbed meditation of the devotee upon his worshipful Lord. The five-year-old devotee Prahlāda Mahārāja also remained mild and composed even while his father tried to torture him, for Prahlāda never forgot the lotus feet of Kṛṣṇa. The *Gītā* compares such peaceful devotees to the ocean: Just as the ocean remains calm though many rivers enter into it; the devotee remains peaceful despite the incessant flow of desires.

Only ecstatic love of God can move the devotee's self-contained, mild nature. The ocean remains calm despite the flowing of thousands of tons or river water, but when the full moon is in the evening sky, then the ocean shores overflood with high tides. Similarly, the mild devotee, when chanting the holy name of Kṛṣṇa, sometimes experiences ecstatic turbulence and sings and dances and cries, without caring for his social appearance.

But within the turbulence of material life the devotee remains calm, because he has reached the supreme objective in life. This is called *ātmārāma,* satisfaction in the self. As a result, a devotee lives a life which doesn't unnecessarily provoke the senses. His habits of eating and sleeping are simple and are maintained only to keep himself healthy for executing devotional service. His regulated, temperate life of eating, drinking, and sleeping helps to produce a non-turbulent, non-violent disposition.

A person who is ingesting quantities of pungent foods, liquors, and intoxicants, whose vision is always agitated by the vapid, mindless images broadcast on television, who is always hearing sex songs and seeing pictures to excite his sex desire, is aflame with passion and sunk in ignorance. Even in the university he is given one speculative process after another without ever reaching a conclusion, and his measure of "learning" is the degree to which his mind is thoroughly agitated and can move constantly from one opinion to another without obtaining a final answer. How can such a person possibly be calm except by the chemically-induced methods of taking coffee, tea, tranquilizers, barbiturates, marijuana, or cocaine, which all produce terrible physical and psychological after-effects and actually drive him further away from a natural, calm disposition?

Besides being agitated by drugs, sense gratification, and mental speculation, such an uncontrolled person occasionally perceives that by his wasted activities he is bring an inauspicious death nearer. He, consequently, sometimes experiences nightmares and other forebodings of evil. The demonic King Kaṁsa, although protected by vast armies, fortresses, weapons, and his own powerful body, had unsettling fears that Kṛṣṇa would one day come and kill him:

> Kaṁsa saw various kinds of inauspicious signs while both awake and dreaming. When he looked in the mirror he could not see his head, although the head was

actually present. He could see the luminaries in the sky in double, although there was only one set factually. He began to see holes in his shadow, and he could hear and high buzzing sound within his ears. All the trees before him appeared to be made of gold, and he could not see his own footprints in the dust or muddy clay. In dreams, he saw various kinds of ghosts being carried in a carriage drawn by donkeys. He also dreamed that someone gave him poison and he was drinking it.

—*Kṛṣṇa,* Vol. II, Ch. 7, p. 35

Another reason the nondevotees are not calm is because of their intense politicking. They are always jockeying for position in some kind of cheating, competitive relationship, either in the big-time arena of professional politics or at their ordinary occupation or among friends and family. Afraid their allies will fail them or their enemies overpower them, they align themselves with various parties for protecting their vested interests. This mentality produces constant anxiety. But as a devotee is surrendered to Kṛṣṇa only, he has not party politics to worry about; he is carefree.

Such was the calm state of the life of Haridāsa Ṭhākura. Even his dwelling place, although simple, reflected his pure state of mind: "Everyone who saw the beauty of the cave [of Haridāsa Ṭhākura], with the *tulasī* plant on a clean altar, was astonished and satisfied at heart." (Cc., *Antya* 3.231) Not only was Haridāsa's cave calm and clean, but his heart and mind were so steadfast and pure than even Māyā devī herself, who came in the form of an alluring woman, could not dissuade Haridāsa from the ecstacy of chanting Hare Kṛṣṇa.

A devotee is also mild in his dealings with others. Of course, the saying is "A Vaiṣṇava is as soft as a rose and as hard as a thunderbolt." So sometimes, when responding to a blasphemous person, for example, he is *not* mild.

Lord Caitanya was not mild when He ran with the *sudarśana cakra* to kill Jagāi and Mādhāi. But the devotee is generally mild in his responses, especially when there is a question of tolerating some wrongdoing against himself. His mild disposition toward events is also compatible with the quality of meekness, or humility. He does not get into a great huff if personally inconvenienced but tends to react mildly, like Haridāsa Ṭhākura in relation to the men who were ordered to cane him in twenty-two marketplaces. That mildness, again, comes not from timidity but from deep self-satisfaction. Like the great ocean, he is pacific. Others get agitated and rant over worldly happenings, personal frustrations, and misgivings, but the devotee depends upon Kṛṣṇa, and tries to carry out His order. Thus a nonviolent, undisturbed, transcendental mildness is another attractive feature of the devotee.

8

A devotee is clean, *śuci.*

Of course, this means clean inside and outside. The devotee's mind, heart, intelligence, body, clothes, living place, place of work, place of worship, his personal and business dealings—all should be *śuci,* clean. "Cleanliness is next to godliness" may be a homely proverb, but it has wisdom for those interested in spiritual life.

When we were just starting the first ISKCON school in 1972, His Divine Grace A. C. Bhaktivedanta Swami Prabhupāda gave us advice stressing cleanliness.

> The future preachers of KC Movement must learn to be suci, absolutely pure in all respects, & for this, practical cleansing is the basic teaching, e.g., not touching anything dirty to mouth. Mouth is dirtiest part, and infection can spread very easily by the mouth. There is word visa-kanya, or the policy of gradually poisoning a beautiful girl so she will adapt ad not be affected, then she will have the potency to assassinate by passing infection by mouth to some enemy. Water itself is most antiseptic, so soap is not always required. The boys should be taught, and also all devotees should also be taught to wash own dishes, hands, mouth—that means always washing. They should be given only what they will eat, so that nothing is left over, and while bathing they can wash their own cloth. Your country, America, will become so much degraded that they will appreciate if we are revolutionary clean.
>
> —Letter to Satsvarūpa dāsa, 2/2/72

A revolution in cleanliness! Even the nondevotee's eating is unclean: flesh and blood, pus from crabs, animals' entrails and brains, fish, pigs, bugs. The meat-eater's diet sound like a witch's brew! He finishes eating and sometimes just wipes his hands across his pants for "cleaning up." The modern bathroom is often equipped with shag carpet on the floor, magazine rack, and electric toothbrush—yet modern man is so primitive in hygiene that after passing stool he doesn't bathe but merely fouls himself with paper and runs a little faucet water over his hands. His uncleanliness in mating needs not be mentioned here.

Kṛṣṇa thus describes the *asuras,* the demoniac: "Neither cleanliness nor proper behavior not truth is found in them." Cleanliness is also one of the four principles of religion, which are presently declining due to the age of Kali. In *Śrīmad-Bhāgavatam* Śrīla Prabhupāda explains:

> The principles of religion do not stand on some dogmas or man-made formulas, but they stand on four primary regulative observances, namely austerity, cleanliness, mercy, and truthfulness. . . . Cleanliness is necessary both for mind and for the body. Simply bodily cleanliness may help to some extent, but cleanliness of the mind is necessary, and it is effected by glorifying the Supreme Lord. No one can cleanse the accumulated mental dust without glorifying the Supreme Lord. A godless civilization cannot cleanse the mind because it has no idea of God, and for this simple reason people under such a civilization cannot have good qualifications, however they may be materially equipped.
>
> —*Bhāg*. 1.17.25, purport

External cleanliness is important, but is has to be done in connection with Kṛṣṇa. The high standard of cleanliness in worshipping the Deity in the temple indicates the worshiper's devotion. *Caitanya-caritāmṛta* gives the account of Rāghava Paṇḍita, who went to great trouble to offer very clean coconuts to Lord Kṛṣṇa in the temple. If there was the slightest discrepancy, Rāghava Paṇḍita would not consider the coconut suitable for offering to the Lord:

> When the coconuts were brought, there was little time to offer them because it was already late. The servant, holding the container of coconuts, remained standing at the door.
>
> Rāghava Paṇḍita saw that the servant touched the ceiling above the door and then touched the coconuts with the same hand.
>
> Rāghava Paṇḍita then said, "People are always coming and going through that door. The dust from their feet blows up and touches the ceiling.
>
> "After touching the ceiling above the door, you have touched the coconuts. Now they are no longer fit to be offered to Kṛṣṇa because they are contaminated."
>
> PURPORT
>
> Śrīla Bhaktisiddhānta Sarasvatī Ṭhākura states that Rāghava Paṇḍita was not simply a crazy fellow suffering from some cleansing phobia. He did not belong to the mundane world. In lower consciousness, accepting something to be spiritual when it is actually material is called *bhauma ijya-dhīḥ*. Rāghava Paṇḍita was an eternal servant of Kṛṣṇa, and everything he saw was related to the service of the Lord. He was always absorbed in the transcendental thought of how he could always serve Kṛṣṇa with everything. Sometimes neophytes, devotees on the lower platform, try to imitate Rāghava Paṇḍita on the platform of material purity and impurity. Such imitation will not help anyone.
>
> —Cc. *Madhya* 15.80–83

In other words, out of pure devotion the devotee wants to make the best and cleanest offering of worship to the Lord. Our spiritual master has encouraged us that when we are cleaning the paraphernalia for the Deity, we are actually cleaning our hearts.

In very recent times the wave of sexual promiscuity has covered the sense of wrong in unclean dealings. According to *Bhagavad-gītā,* sexual affairs, like anything else, should only be utilized in the service of the Supreme. Kṛṣṇa says, "I am sex life according to religious principles." This means that sex should only be within marriage for propagating a child to be raised in God consciousness. Nowadays, the concept that illicit sexual connection is wrong or "dirty" has become outmoded and is considered and old-fashioned naiveté or backwardness. Profanity and obscenity accent the speech of even the most sophisticated persons; in fact, it is considered a mark of sophistication to be able to drop obscene words without a trace of embarrassment. And pornography is literature, films, and other forms of entertainment has become on of the biggest industries in the world, protected by powerful business interests and reverently given freedom by the highest courts of justice. But aside from being a current fashion, illicit and perverted sexual activities will always create deep impurities of the heart. And impure ultimately means against Kṛṣṇa consciousness. Whatever uncleanliness in our minds, hearts, or bodies prevents us from approaching the Supreme Pure, the Supreme Personality of Godhead—such "dirt" is immoral in the most serious way. A morality of cleanliness depends not on puritanical conceptions of right behavior but on becoming pure and clean so that one is suitable to render pure devotional service to the Supreme. Kṛṣṇa has condemned unclean food, unclean sex, and unclean living habits; therefore, a devotee strictly avoids them.

Philosophies other than the philosophy of pure devotional service to the Supreme Personality of Godhead are also unclean. In describing the impersonal conception of liberation, *Śrīmad-Bhāgavatam* uses the phrase *aviśuddha-buddhayaḥ,* "impure intelligence." Desires other than the desire to serve Kṛṣṇa are "dirty things in the heart." Rūpa Gosvāmī, Lord Caitanya's directly empowered disciple, defines devotional service:

anyābhilāṣitā-śunyaṁ
jñāna-karmādy-anāvṛtam
ānukūlyena kṛṣṇānu-
śīlanaṁ bhaktir uttamā

> One should render transcendental loving service to the Supreme Lord Kṛṣṇa favorably and without desire for material profit or gain through fruitive activities or philosophical speculation. That is called pure devotional service.
>
> —*Bhakti-rasāmṛta-sindhu* 1.1.11

Cultivation of knowledge other than pure devotional service, as well as the desire to gain material reward even from religious endeavors, are considered impurities and oppose the conclusion of pure *bhakti. Śrīmad-Bhāgavatam* praises the process of chanting and hearing as being quickly effective in cleansing the heart from all unwanted, dirty things:

> Śrī Kṛṣṇa, the Personality of Godhead, who is the Paramātmā [Supersoul] in everyone's heart and the benefactor of the truthful devotee, cleanses desire for material enjoyment from the heart of the devotee who has developed the urge to hear His messages . . .
>
> —*Bhāg.* 1.2.17

When Nārada Muni was trying to regain the vision of Lord Kṛṣṇa in his meditation, the Lord spoke to him and told him that a devotee had to be completely "free from all material taints" before he could expect to see Him. In this age Lord Caitanya's magnanimous distribution of the chanting of Hare Kṛṣṇa provides us with the most effective method for cleaning the dirty mind and heart and thereby gives us a pure vision of Kṛṣṇa.

An example of the dynamic relationship between outer and inner cleanliness was shown by Lord Caitanya in His pastimes of cleaning the Guṇḍicā temple. As the leader of the Vaiṣṇavas, Lord Caitanya showed not only symbolically but practically the importance of cleanliness. In preparing the temple for the appearance of Lord Jagannātha, Lord Caitanya led the devotees by personally cleaning on His hands and knees. He praised those devotees who collected the most dust, and He chastised those who did not collect enough. Engaging many sweepers, He swept the whole temple and courtyard and then began to wash everything with Ganges water.

Lord Caitanya's devotees splashed water high on the ceilings and walls of the temple, and Caitanya Mahāprabhu Himself wiped the stone altar clean with His own cloth. In his commentary on this section of *Caitanya-caritāmṛta,* Bhaktisiddhānta Sarasvatī takes an internal view of these pastimes and says that unless a devotee makes his own heart perfectly pure of all material taints and desires, then he cannot expect Kṛṣṇa, who is all pure, to appear there.

The political and intellectual leaders of this age are badly lacking in all twenty-six qualities of a Vaiṣṇava, and their lack of cleanliness is easily seen. The country's political leaders claim they want to lead the people and help them, but they actually have other motives in mind. Even at best, the nation's leaders want to engage the people in the cause of nationalism and the pursuit of illusory happiness. The very goals they want the people to strive for and attain are *anarthas,* stumbling blocks on the path of self-realization. Where there is ignorance, an impure heart, an unclean vision—where all is dirty—no one can expect to see purity. And in fact, no one really expects clean dealings even from the president, the father, or the priest.

The Kṛṣṇa consciousness movement is dedicated to making the world "revolutionary clean" through hygienic principles and, even more importantly, by cleansing the heart with the chanting of Hare Kṛṣṇa, Hare Kṛṣṇa, Kṛṣṇa Kṛṣṇa, Hare Hare/ Hare Rāma, Hare Rāma, Rāma Rāma, Hare Hare. When some of Śrīla Prabhupāda's disciples were accused of brainwashing (a charge that was quickly thrown out of court), Śrīla Prabhupāda took the word "brainwashing" in a favorable way and said that was indeed our mission. "Because their brains are filled with stool," he said, "so we have to wash their brains with the chanting of the Lord's names."

As with any one of these Vaiṣṇava qualities, the wonder is that they very soon appear in the activities of even a neophyte devotee. Gradually they will increase more and more, like the waxing moon. The devotee will actually be truthful, he will actually be merciful, and he will actually be clean. Śrīla Prabhupāda had the satisfaction of personally witnessing this transformation in his disciples and he wrote in *Kṛṣṇa, The Supreme Personality of Godhead*:

> During the rainy season, all living entities, in the land, sky and water, become very refreshed, exactly like one

who engages in the transcendental loving service of the Lord. We have practical experience of this with our students in the International Society for Krishna Consciousness. Before becoming students, they were dirty-looking, although they had naturally beautiful personal features; due to having no information of Kṛṣṇa consciousness they appeared very dirty and wretched. Since they have taken to Kṛṣṇa consciousness, their health has improved, and by following the rules and regulations, their bodily luster has increased. When they are dressed with saffron-colored cloth, with *tilaka* on their foreheads and beads in their hands and on their necks, they look exactly as if they have come directly from Vaikuṇṭha.

—*Kṛṣṇa,* Ch. 50

9

A devotee is without material possessions, *akiñcana*.

janmaiśvarya-śruta-śrībhir
edhamāna-madaḥ pumān
naivārhaty abhidhātuṁ vai
tvām akiñcana-gocaram

My Lord, Your Lordship can easily be approached, but only by those who are materially exhausted. One who is on the path of [material] progress, trying to improve himself with respectable parentage, great opulence, high education and bodily beauty, cannot approach You with sincere feeling.

—*Bhāg.* 1.8.26

Sometimes people argue against the total dedication a devotee makes when coming to Kṛṣṇa consciousness. "Why do you have to give up your possessions?" the nondevotee complains. "God doesn't ask that we give up our wealth. He wants us to be happy!" But God *does* ask that we give up our wealth.

Yes, God *does* want us to be happy, and that's why He asks us to give up our wealth. Material possessions will not make us happy. We can be happy only in the eternal, spiritual world, free of the unhappiness of birth, death, disease, and old age. Lord Jesus stresses the same wisdom of renunciation: "It is more difficult for a man attached to wealth to enter the kingdom of God than it is for a camel to enter the eye of a needle!" If we are going to love Kṛṣṇa with our mind, words, and body, then why not with our wealth also?

Surrender of material possessions should be done in the awareness that one is giving up a burden, freeing himself from an entanglement. Material wealth creates an illusion. We put our *faith* in the power of our bank account. We *depend* on our country, our family, or friends. We *love* our material possessions. And in doing so, we cannot feel that Kṛṣṇa is our only shelter. Utter dependence on Kṛṣṇa includes becoming *akiñcana,* materially exhausted. Queen Kuntī therefore addresses Lord Kṛṣṇa as *akiñcana-gocara*. Kṛṣṇa can be achieved by a person who does not put faith in material possessions.

It is for our ultimate good that Kṛṣṇa and Kṛṣṇa's representative tell us to surrender our material possessions. To think that certain riches belong to us is *māyā,* illusion. At the time of death we will have to give up all our possessions; but the *kāma,* the material desiring by which we possess our wealth, will drive us on to another body where we will try again to become happy by material possessions and where we will again suffer the pangs of birth, death, disease, and old age. So as the transcendentalist must learn "I am not this body, I am spirit soul," he must also learn, "The possessions I have accumulated are not mine." Śrīla Prabhupāda explains how material possessions can "intoxicate" a person to the point of making him unable to properly chant the holy name of Kṛṣṇa:

> It is said in the *śāstras* that by once uttering the holy names of the Lord, the sinner gets rid of a quantity of

> sins that he is unable to commit. Such is the power of uttering the holy name of the Lord. There is not the least exaggeration in this statement. Actually, the Lord's holy name has such powerful potency. But there is a quality to such utterances also. It depends on the quality of feeling. A helpless man can feelingly utter the holy name of the Lord, whereas a man who utters the same holy name in great material satisfaction cannot be so sincere.
>
> —*Bhāg.* 1.8.26, purport

Śrīla Prabhupāda has described how elderly men in India renounce family and home and go to Vṛndāvana to spend their last days chanting Hare Kṛṣṇa, yet still they try to keep their wealth. They stay in Vṛndāvana and chant on their beads as long as they are sure that their money remains in the bank or goes to their family members. But Kṛṣṇa, being all-intelligent, sees that the man is still not surrendering. Of course he has come to live as a *bābājī* in Vṛndāvana and call out Kṛṣṇa's names, and that is good; but Kṛṣṇa also wants him to surrender his money.

The materialist cannot understand the simple fact that his dependence on wealth is *māyā*. He does not understand how it is pulling him down into the ocean of birth and death. Having placed his love, faith, and dependence in his wealth, until he offers that wealth at the lotus feet of Kṛṣṇa, he cannot truly live in Vṛndāvana and chant the holy names. Thus foolish persons cling to their few material possessions and give up the real wealth, love of God.

We laugh at the foolishness of an Indian tribe selling Manhattan to the Europeans for twenty-four dollars' worth of trinkets. But in our grasping at the world instead of eternity, bliss, and knowledge, we are being millions of times more foolish. The materialist has sold his soul for trinkets, and he cannot feelingly say, "O Govinda, O Kṛṣṇa. All glories to Rādhā and Kṛṣṇa!" Blinded by the false power of material possessions, he thinks God is for poor people and fools, But he himself soon becomes the poorest of fools. His attachment to material wealth makes him a sure victim for Yamarāja, the Lord of death, and thus he misses the great opportunity of human life—devotional service to Lord Kṛṣṇa. Śrīla Prabhupāda writes, "As long as we have even the slightest tinge of an idea of becoming happy materially in some way or other, we shall have to accept another material body."

The Six Gosvāmīs of Vṛndāvana are classic examples of renunciation in Kṛṣṇa consciousness. Rūpa Gosvāmī and Sanātana Gosvāmī were highly placed government ministers, and Raghunātha dāsa was the son of a very wealthy landowner. They gave up all their material possessions as insignificant and lived in Vṛndāvana wearing only loin cloths and subsisting as mendicants.

It was Rūpa Gosvāmī, however, who enunciated the principle of renunciation through using things in the service of Kṛṣṇa:

anāsaktasya viṣayān
yathārham upayuñjataḥ
nirbandhaḥ kṛṣṇa-sambandhe
yuktaṁ vairāgyam ucyate

prāpañcikatayā buddhyā
hari-sambandhi-vastunaḥ
mumukṣubhiḥ parityāgo
vairāgyaṁ phalgu kathyate

When one is not attached to anything, but at the same time accepts everything in relation to Kṛṣṇa, one is

> rightly situated above possessiveness. On the other hand, one who rejects everything without knowledge of its relationship to Kṛṣṇa is not as complete in his renunciation.
>
> —*Bhakti-rasāmṛta-sindhu* 2.255–256

Śrīla Bhaktisiddhānta Sarasvatī Ṭhākura was the first person to actively preach this dynamic principle of renunciation. Previous to him, Vaiṣṇavas were often thought of as retired to performing solitary *bhajana* in Vṛndāvana. But Bhaktisiddhānta Sarasvatī wanted to create an active worldwide Kṛṣṇa consciousness movement with devotees in the forefront of all activities. The great Vaiṣṇavas of bygone days were often active in the world, although free of material possessiveness. Arjuna and Hanumān are vivid examples of powerful devotees who surrendered everything to Kṛṣṇa and yet performed their devotional service in the field of worldly action. The father of Bhaktisiddhānta Sarasvatī, Bhaktivinoda Ṭhākura, also enunciated the principle of surrendering material possessions by using them in Kṛṣṇa's service.

> All of my possessions—body, brothers, friends, and followers, wife, sons, personal belongings, house and home—all of these I give to You, for I have become Your servant. Now I dwell in Your house. If I continue to maintain my wealth, family members, home and wife, it is because they are Yours. I am a mere servant.
>
> —*Śaraṇāgati, "Ātma-nivedanam,"* 3.1

Of course, one should neither reject nor accept material things whimsically. Only a highly advanced devotee, working directly under the authority of the spiritual master, can know how to keep pace with the material world while remaining pure in consciousness and deed. His Divine Grace A. C. Bhaktivedanta Swami Prabhupāda, following in the footsteps of his spiritual master, used this principle wonderfully in spreading the Kṛṣṇa consciousness movement. Since the cause of Kṛṣṇa consciousness is of the greatest importance for human society, Śrīla Prabhupāda reasoned, why shouldn't the devotees utilize money, land, and whatever is useful for propagating Kṛṣṇa consciousness in the service of the Supreme? It is not that material objects in themselves are evil or lead to repeated birth and death; it is their use outside of direct service to Kṛṣṇa. Śrīla Prabhupāda comments on this in *The Nectar of Devotion:*

> Sometimes people ask us, "Why are you utilizing material products if you condemn the advancement of material civilization?" But actually we do not condemn. We simply ask people to do whatever they are doing in Kṛṣṇa consciousness. This is the same principle on which, in *Bhagavad-gītā,* Kṛṣṇa advised Arjuna to utilize his fighting abilities in devotional service. Similarly, we are utilizing these machines for Kṛṣṇa's service. With such sentiment for Kṛṣṇa, or Kṛṣṇa consciousness, we can accept everything. If the typewriter can be used for advancing our Kṛṣṇa consciousness movement, we must accept it. Similarly the dictating machine or any other machine must be used. Our vision is that Kṛṣṇa is everything. Kṛṣṇa is the cause and effect, and nothing belongs to us. Kṛṣṇa's things must be used in the service of Kṛṣṇa.

Śrīla Prabhupāda envisioned devotional service becoming influential in all fields of society and politics. Bhaktisiddhānta Sarasvatī Ṭhākura used to say that we will know the Kṛṣṇa consciousness movement is successful when we see the high court judge wearing

Vaiṣṇava *tilaka*. This is a far cry from the image of Vaiṣṇavas as those who only sit in a secluded place and chant the holy names. By this higher realization of *akiñcana,* an expert devotee can use anything in Kṛṣṇa's service and thus transform the whole material world into the spiritual world, Vaikuṇṭha.

The underlying axiomatic truth here is that Kṛṣṇa is the Supreme Proprietor. Anyone's claim to own possessions, therefore, is a kind of madness or thievery. As stated in *Īśopaniṣad Mantra* #1, "Everything animate or inanimate that is within the universe is controlled and owned by the Lord. One should therefore accept only those things necessary for himself, which are set aside as his quota, and one should not accept other things, knowing well to whom they belong."

But what is that "quota"? Although the scriptures allow for limited sense gratification and material possessions, that sanction does not constitute pure devotional service. Ultimately Kṛṣṇa's last instruction is to give up even those religious concessions:

sarva-dharmān parityajya
mām ekaṁ śaraṇaṁ vraja
ahaṁ tvāṁ sarva-pāpebhyo
mokṣayiṣyāmi mā śucaḥ

Abandon all varieties of religion and just surrender unto Me. I shall deliver you from all sinful reactions. Do not fear.

—Bg. 18.66

The highest realization then is to see everything as Kṛṣṇa's. The daring, inspired, and compassionate devotee, however, is not satisfied simply to see that it belongs to Kṛṣṇa, but he works to use all things in the service of the Lord—so that the whole world can benefit. Government, art, architecture, economics, science, family—everything should be Kṛṣṇa-ized. In such a spiritualized world society, all the citizens would receive the blessings of Kṛṣṇa, become peaceful and prosperous, and after this life go back home, back to Godhead. So there is dynamic meaning in the concept of *akiñcana,* "being without material possessions."

10

A devotee performs welfare work for everyone, *sarvopakāraka*.

Śrīmad-Bhāgavatam 10.22.35 enjoins: "It is the duty of every living being to perform welfare activities for the benefit of others with his life, wealth, intelligence, and words." The *Viṣṇu Purāṇa* 3.12.45 states: "By his work, thoughts and words, an intelligent man must perform actions which will be beneficial for all living entities in this life and in the next." We have just discussed the ability of the empowered devotee to spiritualize material things in the service of Kṛṣṇa. One who knows the techniques of *bhakti-yoga* can therefore give ultimate benefit to whomever he meets wherever he goes. As the sage Parvata said to Nārada Muni, "You are a touchstone, for by your association even a great hunter has turned into a devotee." In praising the ideal Vaiṣṇava, Sanātana Gosvāmī, Lord Caitanya said, "By the force of your devotional service you purify the whole universe."

The devotee can perform welfare work for everyone, because Kṛṣṇa consciousness applies to all humanity and all species. It is not for only a certain race, nationality, or sex; it is for all living entities. Commenting on the *cātuḥ-ślokī* section of *Śrīmad-Bhāgavatam,* Śrīla Prabhupāda expounds on the universal application of Kṛṣṇa consciousness:

> Śrīla Jīva Gosvāmī Prabhupāda therefore comments on the words *sarvatra sarvadā* in the sense that the principles of *bhakti-yoga,* or devotional service to the Lord, are apt in all circumstances; i.e., *bhakti-yoga* is recommended in all the revealed scriptures, it is performed by all authorities, it is important in all places, it is useful in all causes and effects, etc. . . .
>
> Similarly, the liberty of discharging loving transcendental service to the Lord is invested in everyone, even the women, the *śūdras,* the forest tribes, or any other living beings born into sinful conditions.
>
> —*Bhāg.* 2.9.36, purport

The devotee distributes Kṛṣṇa consciousness to everyone, thus proving its universality. Lord Caitanya has given this duty of distributing Kṛṣṇa consciousness to everyone.

bhārata-bhūmite haila manuṣya-janma yāra
janma sārthaka kari' kara para-upakāra

> One who has taken his birth as a human being in the land of India (Bhārata-varṣa) should make his life successful and work for the benefit of all other people.
>
> —Cc. *Ādi* 9.41

His Divine Grace A. C. Bhaktivedanta Swami Prabhupāda is, without exaggeration, a transcendental worker who stands supreme in the application of *para-upakāra.* (Note that the above verse contains the words *para* and *upakāra,* "benefit for others," which are very similar to *sarvopakāraka.*) For thousands of years the most valuable knowledge of *bhakti-yoga* remained within India. Even Lord Caitanya Mahāprabhu traveled only within India. People outside of Bhārata-varṣa were considered uncivilized *mlecchas.* Even persons who considered themselves Vaiṣṇavas did not think it possible to deliver these fallen *mlecchas*. No devotee could deny the śāstric statements that Kṛṣṇa consciousness should and could apply even to Europeans and Africans, and later to new countries like America, but the śāstric injunction remained theoretical.

Śrīmad-Bhāgavatam states:

kirāta-hūṇāndhra-pulinda-pulkaśā
ābhīra-śumbhā yavanāḥ khasādayaḥ
ye 'nye ca pāpā yad-apāśrayāśrayāḥ
śudhyanti tasmai prabhaviṣṇave namaḥ

> Kirāta, Hūna, Āndhra, Pulinda, Pulkaśa, Ābhīra, Śumbha, Yavana, members of the Khasa races and even others addicted to sinful acts can be purified by taking shelter of the devotees of the Lord, due to His being the supreme power. I beg to offer my respectful obeisances unto Him.
>
> —*Bhāg*. 2.4.18

So this was the śāstric injunction, but who would go to Germany or Russia? How could the African tribesman be elevated? How was it possible? Even Lord Caitanya's explicit statement that devotees spread Kṛṣṇa consciousness worldwide seemed a puzzle.

As late as the early twentieth century, certain Vaiṣṇavas in the Gauḍīya-sampradāya used to ponder over this instruction of Lord Caitanya and wonder whether it was perhaps to be taken symbolically. But His Divine Grace A. C. Bhaktivedanta Swami Prabhupāda has changed all that. Starting single-handedly, arriving in the United States in 1965, he began chanting Hare Kṛṣṇa in New York City and gradually gained a following of young men and women. The Kṛṣṇa consciousness movement, strictly following in disciplic succession from Lord Caitanya Mahāprabhu and Lord Kṛṣṇa, is now teaching this principle of *para-upakara* and is spreading solidly all over the world.

> This is not only the duty of Indians but the duty of everyone, and we are very happy that American and European boys and girls are seriously cooperating with this movement. One should know definitely that the best welfare activity for all of human society is to awaken man's God consciousness, or Kṛṣṇa consciousness. Therefore, everyone should help this great movement.
>
> —Cc. *Ādi* 9.41, purport

Both *Śrīmad-Bhāgavatam* and Lord Caitanya Mahāprabhu emphasize that pure devotional service to Kṛṣṇa is open to people of all social orders all over the world. In carrying out the spirit of this all-embracing *bhakti-yoga* movement, Śrīla Prabhupāda created *brāhmaṇas* from those who were born and raised as meat-eaters. Thus Śrīla Prabhupāda proved that devotional service was all-powerful welfare work and that it should be given to the most fallen. Some caste conscious Hindus objected to Śrīla Prabhupāda giving second initiation and the sacred thread to Westerners, but these critics could not support their criticisms with *śāstra*. Statements like the following assertion by Nārada Muni testify in defense of Śrīla Prabhupāda's work:

yasya yal lakṣaṇaṁ proktaṁ
puṁso varṇābhivyañjakam
yad anyatrāpi dṛśyeta
tat tenaiva vinirdiśet

> If one shows the symptoms of being a *brāhmaṇa, kṣatriya, vaiśya* or *śūdra,* as described above, even if he has appeared in a different class, he should be accepted according to those symptoms of classification.
>
> —*Bhāg*. 7.11.35

Hari-bhakti-vilāsa, Sanātana Gosvāmī's guide book for the Vaiṣṇavas, gives further evidence:

yathā kāñcanatāṁ yāti
kāṁsyaṁ rasa-vidhānataḥ
tathā dīkṣā-vidhānena
dvijatvaṁ jāyate nṛṇām

> As bell metal is turned to gold when mixed with mercury in an alchemical process, so one who is properly trained and initiated by a bona fide spiritual master immediately becomes a *brāhmaṇa.*
>
> —*Hari-bhakti-vilāsa,* 2.12

Śrīla Prabhupāda also created *sannyāsīs* and gurus. More objections came, but he defended his actions with *śāstra.* Again and again, Śrīla Prabhupāda cited Vedic evidence to support his activities and also pointed to the good behavior of his sincere disciples, who are actually free from illicit sex, meat-eating, intoxication, and gambling, who are chanting sixteen rounds daily of the Hare Kṛṣṇa mantra, and who are fully engaged in Kṛṣṇa conscious service. Prabhupāda pointed out the theoretical *and* practical evidence: by chanting Hare Kṛṣṇa even those born in sinful families could come to the level of the Vaiṣṇava. Śrīla Prabhupāda, while narrating the story of Nārada Muni instructing Dhruva Mahārāja to chant the Vedic mantras and worship the Deity, took the opportunity to explain his worldwide preaching:

> Our Kṛṣṇa consciousness movement is going on throughout the entire world, and we also install Deities in different centers. Sometimes our Indian friends, puffed up with concocted notions, criticize, "This has not been done. That has not been done" But they forget this instruction of Nārada Muni to one of the greatest Vaiṣṇavas, Dhruva Mahārāja. One has to consider the particular time, country and conveniences. What is convenient in India may not be convenient in Western countries. Those who are not actually in the line of *ācāryas,* or who personally have no knowledge of how to act in the role of *ācārya,* unnecessarily criticize the activities of the ISKCON movement in countries outside of India. The fact is that such critics cannot do anything personally to spread Kṛṣṇa consciousness. If someone does go and preach, taking all risks and allowing all considerations for time and place, it might be that there are changes in the manner of worship, but that is not at all faulty according to *śāstra.* Śrīman Vīrarāghava Ācārya, an *ācārya* in the disciplic succession of the Rāmānuja-*sampradāya,* has remarked in his commentary that *caṇḍālas,* or conditioned souls who are born in lower than *śūdra* families, can also be initiated according to circumstances. The formalities may be slightly changed here and there to make them Vaiṣṇavas.
>
> Lord Caitanya Mahāprabhu recommends that His name should be heard in every nook and corner of the world. How is this possible unless one preaches everywhere? . . . By this process the entire world can be converted to Kṛṣṇa consciousness.
>
> —*Bhāg.* 4.8.54, purport

Another example of Śrīla Prabhupāda's universal vision was his welcoming women into the ranks of the International Society for Krishna Consciousness. Predictably, caste conscious Hindus objected. But on what śāstric or philosophical basis could women be denied an equal chance to take to Kṛṣṇa consciousness? Lord Kṛṣṇa had affirmed in *Bhagavad-gītā*:

māṁ hi pārtha vyapāśritya
ye 'pi syuḥ pāpa-yonayaḥ
striyo vaiśyās tathā śūdrās
te 'pi yānti parāṁ gatim

O son of Pṛthā, those who take shelter in Me, though they be of lower birth—women, *vaiśyas* (merchants), and *śūdras* (workers)—can attain the supreme destination.
—Bg. 9.32

Śrīla Prabhupāda explained that his allowing women to become initiated disciples, preachers, and temple attendants did not mean he allowed illicit sex. *Caitanya-caritāmṛta Ādi* 7.38 says: "Śrī Caitanya Mahāprabhu appeared in order to deliver all the fallen souls. Therefore He devised many methods to liberate them from the clutches of *māyā*." In a purport Śrīla Prabhupāda states:

Not knowing that boys and girls in countries like Europe and America mix very freely, these fools and rascals criticize the boys and girls in Kṛṣṇa consciousness for intermingling. But these rascals should consider that one cannot suddenly change a community's social customs. However, since both the boys and girls are being trained to become preachers, those girls are not ordinary girls but are as good as their brothers who are preaching Kṛṣṇa consciousness. Therefore, to engage both boys and girls in fully transcendental activities is a policy intended to spread the Kṛṣṇa consciousness movement. These jealous fools who criticize the intermingling of boys and girls will simply have to be satisfied with their own foolishness because they cannot think of how to spread Kṛṣṇa consciousness by adopting ways and means that are favorable for this purpose.

—Cc. *Ādi* 7.31–32

Sometimes those who are supposed to be followers of Hinduism say that the Vedic message of liberation is not to be spread. They say because Vedic knowledge is spiritual or mystical, every person has to find it on his own; preaching will do no good. But this is another concoction, unsupported by the *śāstra*. Although the Supreme Lord created this material world for the illusory enjoyment of the living entities, He has, nevertheless, since the dawn of creation, propagated the message of returning back to home, back to Godhead. Each of the many incarnations of the Lord descend to deliver this message. Those who are sincere sons and devotees of the Supreme and who understand the purport of the *śāstra* assist Lord Kṛṣṇa in His mission. Lord Kṛṣṇa recognizes these workers in the *Bhagavad-gītā*:

ya idaṁ paramaṁ guhyaṁ
mad-bhakteṣv abhidhāsyati
bhaktiṁ mayi parāṁ kṛtvā
mām evaiṣyaty asaṁśayaḥ

na ca tasmān manuṣyeṣu
kaścin me priya-kṛttamaḥ
bhavitā na ca me tasmād
anyaḥ priyataro bhuvi

For one who explains the supreme secret to the devotees, pure devotional service is guaranteed, and at the end he will come back to Me. There is no servant in this world more dear to Me than he, nor will there ever be one more dear.

—Bg. 18.68–69

The Vedic literature states, *yasmin tuṣṭe jagat tuṣṭam:* "If the Supreme Personality of Godhead is satisfied, everyone is satisfied." But here we see from the *Gītā* verses above that Kṛṣṇa is satisfied when His sincere devotees actively spread his message. Kṛṣṇa was not satisfied when Arjuna wanted just to sit on the chariot. Although Kṛṣṇa was Arjuna's dear friend, Arjuna did not say, "Kṛṣṇa, You are my friend, so You do the fighting while I sit here." Instead, Kṛṣṇa preached vigorously to Arjuna, inciting him to take action against the enemy. Arjuna satisfied Kṛṣṇa, and the Lord was pleased to defeat the vast armies of Dhṛtarāṣṭra. Kṛṣṇa actually did the killing, but Arjuna got the credit, because he exerted his full will and effort in the service of the Lord. Kṛṣṇa wants His message of "back home, back to Godhead" spread all over the world, and He wants it done by the vigorous activities of devotees preaching on His behalf.

Aside from sectarian Hindus, those who are agnostic and atheistic also challenge the Vaiṣṇava's claim to be a welfare worker. They want to know, "What are you doing to help the poor, politically oppressed? What's your claim to being a welfare worker?" They think devotional service merely sentimental. In answer to this, Kṛṣṇadāsa Kavirāja, author of *Caitanya-caritāmṛta,* invites intelligent men to apply their arguments and logic to understanding the humanitarian work of Lord Caitanya. "If you are indeed interested in logic and argument, kindly apply it to the mercy of Śrī Caitanya Mahāprabhu. If you do so, you will find it to be strikingly wonderful." (Cc. *Ādi* 8.15)

I have already discussed under the quality of "mercifulness" that there is no real mercy without Kṛṣṇa consciousness. People are suffering in the material world due to their karma, and one cannot alleviate the suffering simply by material adjustments. Usually people engage in humanitarian activities on the basis of the body. But the material body is ultimately subject to destruction, whereas the spiritual soul is eternal. Lord Caitanya's philanthropic activities are performed in connection with the eternal soul. Whatever benefit one can give to this body, politically, socially, or medically, is only a patchwork solution. In the end, the body will be destroyed, and one will have to accept another body according to his life's activities. If a person does not understand the science of transmigration and takes his body to be the self, then he is in ignorance. And any welfare worker who gives no information on these facts of life is a cheater. Lord Caitanya Mahāprabhu's program, while not neglecting material necessities, stresses on spiritual necessities, the real need of human society.

An example of the extreme munificence of a devotee desiring the welfare of others is seen in the lives of Haridāsa Ṭhākura and Vāsudeva Datta, two followers of Lord Caitanya. Lord Caitanya confided in Haridāsa Ṭhākura regarding His anxiety to deliver *yavanas* (persons against the Vedic principles). Haridāsa Ṭhākura assured Lord Caitanya that the *yavanas* would be saved by their inadvertent chanting of the holy names of God. A devotee in ecstatic love chants "*hā rāma*" ("O my Lord Rāmacandra"), and the *yavanas* also chant "*hā rāma,*" taking it to mean something else. By this accidental chanting of the holy name, Haridāsa Ṭhākura said, the *yavanas* would be saved. Haridāsa Ṭhākura then informed Lord Caitanya that, by the Lord's holding loud *saṅkīrtana,* all the moving and nonmoving living entities had already been delivered. And in the future the deliverance of the *yavanas* would be carried out by those in succession from Lord Caitanya.

Haridāsa Ṭhākura said, "When loud chanting of the Hare Kṛṣṇa mantra is performed all over the world by those who follow in the Your footsteps, all the living entities, moving and nonmoving, dance in ecstatic devotional love."

On another occasion Vāsudeva Datta approached Lord Caitanya with a request. He said he was very aggrieved to see the suffering of all conditioned souls. "I request You," said Vāsudeva Datta, "to transfer the karma of their sinful lives upon my head." Being fully prepared to accept the sins of everyone in the universe and to suffer all their reactions, Vāsudeva Datta demonstrated an inconceivable desire for other's welfare. He was willing to risk everything to rescue the conditioned souls from material existence. With great feeling, Lord Caitanya then explained that simply by Vāsudeva Datta's desiring, Kṛṣṇa would deliver the living entities. In response to the wishes of His pure devotee, the Supreme Lord can easily deliver the whole world.

This same mood of praying to Kṛṣṇa to deliver all the conditioned souls was expressed by the personified *Vedas,* who prayed to Mahā-Viṣṇu at the beginning of creation. Creation means that the conditioned souls enter into the material world under the influence of *māyā,* but the personified *Vedas* prayed for the Lord to show His mercy by attracting the conditioned souls back home, back to Godhead:

> O my Lord, O unconquerable one, O master of all potencies, please exhibit Your internal potency to conquer the nescience of all moving and inert living entities. Due to nescience, they accept all kinds of faulty things, thus provoking a fearful situation. O Lord, please show Your glories! You can do this very easily, for Your internal potency is beyond the external

> potency, and You are the reservoir of all opulence. You are also the demonstrator of the material potency. You are also always engaged in Your pastimes in the spiritual world, where You exhibit Your reserved, internal potency, and sometimes You exhibit the external potency by glancing over it. Thus You manifest Your pastimes. The Vedas confirm Your two potencies and accept both types of pastimes due to them.
>
> —*Kṛṣṇa,* "The Prayers of the Personified Vedas"

The good wishes, prayers, intentions, and self-sacrificing activities of the devotee bring about immense good for all persons in the material world. The devotees are rarely celebrated for this work while within the material world, but they are very dear to Kṛṣṇa. We are all indebted to the true humanitarian workers, the devotees of the Lord.

11

A devotee is peaceful, *śānta*.

Some of the twenty-six qualities appear to be quite similar. I have already discussed "mild," which is close in meaning to "peaceful," and I shall also discuss "desireless," which is the main basis for peacefulness. Also I have discussed "without material possessions," and I shall later discuss "indifference to material acquisitions." "Mercifulness" has been discussed and its near-synonym, "compassion," is yet to come. So there are often fine distinctions in the various meanings, with some overlapping and repetition. But this indicates that certain traits are an especially important part of a devotee's character. I will present these similar qualities strictly in *paramparā* but from different angles of vision.

A devotee is peaceful because he realizes that Kṛṣṇa is everything. There is a common expression, "Make peace with God." This implies that one is "warring" with God and that he cannot become peaceful until he makes peace with the Supreme. This is correct. We have to make peace with Kṛṣṇa; then we can make peace with ourselves, with our body, with others, and with the whole universe. And we can remain peaceful even in times of distress.

To make peace with God we first must know who He is and what His position is. *Bhagavad-gītā* describes this knowledge: *vāsudevaḥ sarvam iti,* or "Kṛṣṇa is everything." Kṛṣṇa says this understanding can only be attained after many lifetimes of researching the Absolute Truth. "That *mahatma* is very rare" who realizes Kṛṣṇa is everything. This is far more than merely admitting that God exists; it is the realization that nothing exists except Kṛṣṇa and that therefore one should live one's life in full devotion to Him. To think there is anything outside of Kṛṣṇa or to make plans to enjoy apart from Him is illusion and cannot make us happy or peaceful.

In *Śrīmad-Bhāgavatam* 1.5.14, Nārada Muni, in speaking to his disciple Śrīla Vyāsadeva, states, "Whatever you desire to describe that is separate in vision from the Lord simply reacts, with different forms, names, and results, to agitate the mind as the wind agitates a boat which has no resting place." If we fail to accept Kṛṣṇa as the basis of all reality, then our minds remain restless and disturbed, like a lost boat at sea.

Lord Kṛṣṇa gives us this information in *Bhagavad-gītā*:

bhoktāraṁ yajña-tapasāṁ
sarva-loka-maheśvaram
suhṛdaṁ sarva-bhūtānāṁ
jñātvā māṁ śāntim ṛcchati

> A person in full consciousness of Me, knowing Me to be the ultimate beneficiary of all sacrifices and austerities, the Supreme Lord of all planets and demigods, and the benefactor and well-wisher of all living entities, attains peace from the pangs of material miseries.
> —Bg. 5.29

Śrīla Prabhupāda calls this verse "the peace formula." We say "God is everything," but here are three important realizations about God: (1) whatever work we do is actually meant to be offered unto Him; (2) the Supreme Personality of Godhead is the owner and controller of all the planets, and men and nations should not claim they are proprietors; (3) Kṛṣṇa is the friend of all living beings. One who acknowledges these three attributes of Kṛṣṇa and who serves and worships Him "attains peace from the pangs of material miseries."

The first attribute of Kṛṣṇa described in the "peace formula" verse is that He is "the ultimate purpose of all sacrifices and austerities." We should do everything for Kṛṣṇa; that is our constitutional nature. As spirit souls, we are eternal fragments of God. Everything is Kṛṣṇa—manifested in different expansions. Kṛṣṇa is the root of the complete tree, the stomach of the complete body. As pouring water on the root is the right process to water the tree, as feeding the stomach supplies energy to all parts of the body, so the part-and-parcel living entity becomes satisfied only when he acts in a favorable relation to the whole.

Sometimes we hear psychologists speak of self-realization or self-actualization, but *this* is absolute self-realization: consciousness that we are an individual self in an eternal relationship of loving service to Kṛṣṇa. It is in that spirit that Kṛṣṇa advises in *Bhagavad-gītā* 9.27, "Whatever you do, whatever you eat, whatever you offer or give away, and whatever austerities you perform—do that, O son of Kuntī, as an offering to Me." Everyone has to render some work to survive in this world, but such prescribed duties should be done as an offering to Kṛṣṇa. Devotional work offered to Kṛṣṇa is known as *yajña* (sacrifice). Unless we do our work as *yajña,* we will be entangled in the reactions of *karma.*

It is not only our duty and constitutional position to work for Kṛṣṇa and make Him the beneficiary, but it is the prime source of bliss and satisfaction for the soul. Concerning the happy results of *yajña,* Lord Kṛṣṇa promises:

> In the beginning of creation, the Lord of all creatures sent forth generations of men and demigods along with sacrifices for Viṣṇu, and blessed them by saying, "Be thou happy by this *yajña* (sacrifice) because its performance will bestow upon you everything desirable for living happily and achieving liberation.
>
> —Bg. 3.10

As the source of everything, Kṛṣṇa awards the pious man with material goods. But beyond this, the eternal pleasure of the spirit soul is in serving Kṛṣṇa as the beneficiary of all our occupational or religious acts:

> The supreme occupation (*dharma*) for all humanity is that by which men can attain to loving devotional service unto the transcendent Lord. Such devotional service must be unmotivated and uninterrupted to completely satisfy the self.
>
> —*Bhāg*. 1.2.6

We have to give up once and for all the ridiculous pretense of being the supreme enjoyer and recognize the reality of the almighty Godhead. To come to this awakened state of recognizing that we are part and parcel of God and that we should serve Him brings certain peace.

Also included in the "peace formula" is that Kṛṣṇa is the proprietor of all the worlds. As soon as we think, therefore, that we own something, we become thieves. A thief is always in anxiety that the police may catch him at any moment and throw him into jail, or like the bank robber, John Dillinger, that he may be shot on sight by the police. Of course, one may be a thief, taking Kṛṣṇa's property for himself, and be respected by the state, but ultimately he will be punished by the most powerful police force, the agents of *māyā*.

To claim ownership without any reference to the supreme proprietor, Kṛṣṇa, is a fraud. A house, for example, is made from materials like earth, wood, stone, and iron—all raw materials provided by the material nature under the control of the Supreme. If a man brings together these elements and shapes them by his labor, is he their ultimate owner? Within a few years, death forces him to leave the building of his so-called proprietorship. Once the native American Indians owned the land that is now the United States, and in the future another group may own it. Clearly, man's actual position is that he is being given use of land and other commodities by a higher authority and ownership. No state, neither capitalist nor communist, is the true owner of any part of this planet; everything is the property of Kṛṣṇa.

Placing the "peace formula" into crucial relevance for the modern day, Prabhupāda explains the alternatives that are open for humanity:

> Nuclear bombs are in the hands of both communists and capitalists, and if both do not recognize the proprietorship of the Supreme Lord, it is certain that these bombs will ultimately ruin both parties. Thus in order to save themselves and bring peace to the world, both parties must follow the instructions of *Śrī Īśopaniṣad.*
>
> —*Śrī Īśopaniṣad, Mantra* #1, purport

The gross materialist cannot conceive of the glorious destination of God's servants. He thinks that to become a servant is demeaning. But to be a servant of Kṛṣṇa is the most wonderful thing. "Become great by serving the great," Śrīla Prabhupāda would say. In the spiritual world the eternal servants of Kṛṣṇa share almost all the opulences of the Supreme Personality of Godhead, and yet they always render Him eternal, loving service. And in the material world Lord Kṛṣṇa, the Supreme Personality, is the patron of His devotees, so they have nothing to fear. Thinking that any person or nation or power is the controller beyond Kṛṣṇa can never bring peace. Peace comes when we recognize that everything belongs to the Supreme.

According to the "peace formula," Lord Kṛṣṇa is also described as the dearmost friend of all living beings. That God is all-powerful does not mean that He is an enemy whom everyone has to bow to out of fear. He is our closest friend; He is in everyone's heart; and only He knows our suffering and our worth. A man or woman cannot be our best friend. Many "friends" are not even well-intentioned. Even if they are, they cannot help us at the time of death. A friend can commiserate with us, but Kṛṣṇa can help us out of all difficulty. A real friend in this world is he who tells us, "Kṛṣṇa is your friend." As Arjuna's friend, Kṛṣṇa is the ideal chivalrous comrade, the best intimate confidant, and the supreme spiritual master. In Kṛṣṇaloka, Kṛṣṇa sports with His transcendental pals in His original childhood form, without any formality or reverence, but in pure love. We each have a unique, eternal relationship, or *rasa,* with Kṛṣṇa. But regardless of that *rasa,* Kṛṣṇa is the friend of all—devotee or nondevotee. We simply have to turn to Him. Kṛṣṇa promises, "I envy no one, nor am I partial to anyone. I am equal to all. But whoever renders service unto Me in devotion is a friend, is in Me, and I am also a friend to him." (Bg. 9.29)

Once we make peace with God, then we can also be peaceful with ourselves. Speculators say that one can be happy when he indulges himself or tries to understand himself as a unique person—without reference to devotional service. But such speculators don't know the actual self.

It is not that each person has to go on an individual search to find out his basic identity. The identity of each self is fixed as the eternal part and parcel of Kṛṣṇa. By chanting the names of Kṛṣṇa a person realizes his unique relationship with Kṛṣṇa.

Not to know yourself is certainly a serious dilemma; if you don't know who you are, then how can you be happy? But the process of self-realization, the process that brings self-knowledge and peace, is *bhakti-yoga*. We have to link up with Kṛṣṇa in service, then we will know who we are. Free from ignorance of the self, we can finally be free and happy. Śrīla Prabhupāda describes satisfaction of the self.

> The need of the spirit soul is that he wants to get out of the limited sphere of material bondage and fulfill his desire for complete freedom. He wants to get out of the covered walls of the greater universe. He wants to see the free light and the spirit. That complete freedom is achieved when he meets the complete spirit, the Personality of Godhead.
>
> —*Bhāg*. 1.2.8, purport

Making peace with God automatically includes making peace with the self as well as with the body. When we try to become happy through the senses of the material body, we fall into great distress. For example, people base their life's satisfaction on sex pleasure; but after a few short years the body grows too old to enjoy. Then what? Seeking satisfaction through sex and other material, bodily pleasures, we meet frustration at every turn, until finally everything is destroyed by encroaching death. There is an inherent anxiety for the soul who, in ignorance, takes his body to be his very self. A person in bodily consciousness is in a precarious situation; even if he denies it, unconsciously he is afraid that at any moment he may be dashed in oblivion. A devotee, however, understands that the real self is different from the body, and therefore he can come to peaceful terms with his body. He understands that the demands of the body should be neither neglected nor exaggerated. This is described in *Śrīmad-Bhāgavatam.*

> Life's desires should never be directed towards sense gratification. One should desire only a healthy life, or self-preservation, since a human being is meant for inquiry about the Absolute Truth. Nothing else should be the goal of one's works.
>
> —*Bhāg.* 1.2.10

Bhagavad-gītā describes the human body metaphorically as a city of nine gates. (The nine gates refer to the nine natural openings of the body. mouth, ears, etc.) Kṛṣṇa says that a person in the mode of goodness lives happily within the city of nine gates, whereas one in passion or ignorance suffers various distresses and ailments. A devotee does not pamper his body with excessive eating or sleeping, nor does he unnecessarily deny the body these things. A devotee regards the body as a temple of the Lord, because the Supersoul is transcendentally situated in the heart along with the soul. Using his body as an instrument for serving Kṛṣṇa, the devotee tends it in a regulated way, living a peaceful, regulated life. Thus his body is peaceful. And if there is disruption, as will naturally occur within the material world, the devotee takes it for what it is. He does not become confused about distresses of the body, knowing they are temporary. Both pleasures and pains he learns to endure. He is peaceful, not giving in to the demands of the body.

A devotee is also peaceful in his dealings with others. He has no quarrel. He depends on Kṛṣṇa and is not involved in the struggles for existence, nor is he after another's possessions. This is the basis for brotherly love. As a brother cooperates with another brother, so all humanity can cooperate by realizing the Supreme Father as the center of existence. Peacefulness, according to the Kṛṣṇa conscious formula, is beneficial for all people in all parts of the world. Peace can be reached not by political manipulations but only by recognizing Kṛṣṇa.

In the 1940s, before the formation of the United Nations after World War II, Śrīla Prabhupāda began his journal, *Back to Godhead.* He wrote and preached actively, addressing himself to world leaders. At that time just after the war, leaders of many nations expressed a weary cynicism as to whether this world war might not be followed by another. Everyone was anxious for peace—but how to insure it? In many articles and letters to world leaders, Prabhupāda pointed out that war was a karmīc reaction to humanity's misdeeds. Unless leaders and nations acted with reference to Kṛṣṇa—the ultimate beneficiary of all acts, the Supreme Lord of all the universes, and the best friend of all humanity—war would surely follow like a law of nature. Prabhupāda wrote that never by their own devices could men escape the conditions of destruction. So many world leaders were seeking relief from the war, but their measures would all prove useless because their attempts for peace were within a material conception of life. Their attempts were like trying to alleviate darkness with darkness. Peace—international, national, familial, self—is possible only through following the merciful instruction of Kṛṣṇa and Kṛṣṇa's representative. "One who is not in transcendental consciousness can have neither a controlled mind nor steady intelligence, without which there is no possibility of peace. And how can there be any happiness without peace?" (Bg. 2.66)

The dictionary defines *peaceful* as "undisturbed by strife, turmoil, or disagreement." Of course, it is impossible to find a place or situation in the material world that is completely tranquil. To be peaceful, therefore, one must be undisturbed despite the presence of strife and turmoil. *Bhagavad-gītā* explains this criterion of transcendental consciousness:

> In that joyous state, one is situated in boundless transcendental happiness, realized through transcendental senses. Established thus, one never departs from the truth, and upon gaining this he thinks there is no greater gain. Being situated in such a position, one is never shaken even in the midst of the greatest difficulty.
>
> —Bg. 6.21–23

So *peaceful* does not refer to a physically idyllic setting that may in fact be shattered at any moment. *Peaceful* is the condition of the soul at peace with Kṛṣṇa, and it is possible for the devotee who sees Kṛṣṇa as everything. Śrīla Prabhupāda writes in *Bhagavad-gītā,* "Realization that there is no existence besides Kṛṣṇa is the platform of peace and fearlessness."

Kṛṣṇa consciousness means that a devotee can always think of Kṛṣṇa and chant Hare Kṛṣṇa whether he is in heaven or hell. This rare peacefulness is the blessing of Kṛṣṇa for whoever sincerely enters His devotional service and gives up the unpeaceful world of material desires.

12

A devotee is surrendered to Kṛṣṇa, *kṛṣṇaika-śaraṇa.*

This quality of the Vaiṣṇava is explicitly devotional. The Sanskrit words *kṛṣṇa-eka,* "only to Kṛṣṇa," and *śaraṇa,* "surrendered to," are clear and to the point. Although "mercifulness," "truthfulness," and other qualities are also strictly in relation to Kṛṣṇa, with "*kṛṣṇaika-śaraṇa*" the connection is transparent and the meaning saturated with *bhakti.*

And yet there are impersonalist philosophers—the Māyāvādīs—who would try to misinterpret *kṛṣṇaika-śaraṇa* and mislead others away from Kṛṣṇa. Once when a Hinduism professor visited Śrīla Prabhupāda, Prabhupāda asked him, "What is Hinduism?" When the Hinduism professor replied, "I do not know," Prabhupāda said, "You mean you are teaching Hinduism, but you don't even know what it is?" The professor confessed that Hinduism was so complex and many-branched that he didn't know how to describe it. Śrīla Prabhupāda then explained how the word "Hindu" is a misnomer, and that the real purpose of the Vedic literature is to educate the human being about his relationship with the Absolute Truth, the Personality of Godhead. Prabhupāda cited *Bhagavad-gītā*:

sarva-dharmān parityajya
mām ekaṁ śaraṇaṁ vraja

ahaṁ tvāṁ sarva-pāpebhyo
mokṣayiṣyāmi mā śucaḥ

Abandon all varieties of religion and just surrender unto Me. I shall deliver you from all sinful reactions. Do not fear.

—Bg. 18.66

The Hinduism professor, rather than accept the conclusion of *Bhagavad-gītā,* asked Prabhupāda if he could give an etymological meaning of the word *śaraṇa*m. Prabhupāda replied simply, "*Śaraṇam* means 'surrender'" The professor became argumentative. He did not want to accept the conclusion that Kṛṣṇa is everything and that the goal of Vedic or Hindu culture is to understand Him. He insisted Prabhupāda give a different etymological explanation of *śaraṇa*m. When Prabhupāda again replied that *śaraṇa*m means surrender, the professor explained, "No, no. That is a definition. I asked you for the etymology. What is the root? What is the history of this word?" Seeing that his guest was uninterested in hearing submissively, Prabhupāda said that for root explanations of words the professor would do better to talk with a Sanskrit scholar instead of a spiritual master. Since Śrīla Prabhupāda's expertise in translating *Śrīmad-Bhāgavatam* and *Bhagavad-gītā* has been praised by Sanskrit professors around the world, we should not think his straightforward definition of the word *śaraṇa*m was incorrect or unscholarly. There are always those who, not wanting to surrender to Kṛṣṇa, evade the issue on the pretext of scholarship.

The Māyāvādīs also contest the word "Kṛṣṇa." One well-known scholar tried to evade Kṛṣṇa in his commentary on the following verse from *Bhagavad-gītā*:

man-manā bhava mad-bhakto
mad-yājī māṁ namaskuru
mām evaiṣyasi yuktvaivam
ātmānaṁ mat-parāyaṇaḥ

Engage your mind always in thinking of Me, become My devotee, offer obeisances to Me, and worship Me. Being completely absorbed in Me, surely you will come to Me.

—Bg. 9.34

The meaning is clear; the Sanskrit is not ambiguous. But this commentator says it's not to Kṛṣṇa that we have to surrender but to the impersonal principle *within* Kṛṣṇa. By making a distinction between the inside and outside of Kṛṣṇa, this speculative philosopher exposes his ignorance of the true nature of the Personality of Godhead. As stated in the *Kurma Purāṇa, deha dehi vibhedo 'yam neśvare vidyate kvacit:* "In the Supreme Lord, Kṛṣṇa, there is no difference between Himself and His body." Everything about Kṛṣṇa—His body, His mind, and He Himself—are one and absolute. Because the Sanskrit name *Kṛṣṇa* bears different etymological meanings, Māyāvādī philosophers have made absurd endeavors to misinterpret the holy name. But the fact remains that the name Kṛṣṇa is identical with the Supreme Personality of Godhead, the cause of all causes.

Kṛṣṇa consciousness is simple for those who are pure, but difficult for the crooked. Knowledge of Kṛṣṇa is presented throughout the *Vedas* and is taught by the great *ācāryas*. Lord Caitanya's immediate followers, the Six Gosvāmīs, scrutinizingly studied all the revealed scriptures with the aim of presenting Kṛṣṇa as the cause of all causes, and the object of all worship. In *Bhagavad-gītā*, the most widely accepted and respected of all Vedic literatures, the speaker is Śrī Kṛṣṇa Himself, and He reveals, "There is no truth higher than Me. Everything comes from Me." *Śrīmad-Bhāgavatam* 1.3.28 gives the same conclusion: *ete cāṁṣa-kalāḥ puṁsaḥ, kṛṣṇas tu bhagavān svayam.* "All of the above-mentioned incarnations of God are either plenary portions or portions of the plenary portions of the Lord, but Lord Śrī Kṛṣṇa is the original Personality of Godhead."

Śrīla Bhaktisiddhānta Sarasvatī once made an extensive compilation of Kṛṣṇa's attributes, all taken from *Śrīmad-Bhāgavatam's* Tenth Canto. Here are some of them:

Kṛṣṇa is inaccessible to sensuous knowledge (16/46)
Kṛṣṇa is Lord of the infinity of worlds (69/17)
Kṛṣṇa wields the power of creating the unlimited (87/28)
Kṛṣṇa carries the impress of limitless power (87/14)
Kṛṣṇa is possessed of inconceivable potency (10/29)
Kṛṣṇa is unborn (59/28, 74/21)
Kṛṣṇa is vanquished by exclusive devotion (14/3)
Kṛṣṇa is Inner Guide (1/7)
Kṛṣṇa is Primal God (40/1)
Kṛṣṇa is Primal Person, Puruṣa (63/38)
Kṛṣṇa is overwhelming flood of bliss (83/4)
Kṛṣṇa is dispeller of the night of pseudo-religion (14/40)
Kṛṣṇa is the only truth (14/23)
Kṛṣṇa is the Person who is time (1/7)
Kṛṣṇa is Time's Own Self (70/26)
Kṛṣṇa is even the Time of time (56/27)
Kṛṣṇa is present in the heart of every animate entity like fire inside wood (46/36)
Kṛṣṇa is destroyer of the pride of the arrogant (60/19)
Kṛṣṇa is the cause of the world (4/1)

Kṛṣṇa is the creator of the world (70/38)
Kṛṣṇa appears as if possessed of a body like that of mundane entities, for the good of the world (14/55)
Kṛṣṇa is the Guru (center of gravity) of the world (80/44)
Kṛṣṇa is the destroyer of the miseries of persons who employ themselves in meditating upon Him (58/10)
Kṛṣṇa is the God of gods (80/44)
Kṛṣṇa's presence mocks the world of man (70/40)
Kṛṣṇa is the manifester of all light (63/34)
Kṛṣṇa is unstinted in giving Himself away to one who remembers Him (80/11)

We can judge our advancement in Kṛṣṇa consciousness by our attraction to hear about Kṛṣṇa and to render devotional service unto Him. The science of Kṛṣṇa is unfathomable, but preliminary recognition of Kṛṣṇa as the Supreme Person is not difficult.

Surrender to Kṛṣṇa is also not difficult to understand or to execute. According to Lord Caitanya, a person has four things he can surrender: his life, his wealth, his intelligence, and his words. Complete surrender is to give one's whole life. If someone can't do that, then he can at least give some of his wealth or intelligence or words. Studying *Bhagavad-gītā* is surrender of one's intelligence to Kṛṣṇa; speaking something favorable about Kṛṣṇa is surrender of words.

We cannot surrender unless we are free of pride (Bg. 15.5, purport). Surrender begins by surrendering to the spiritual master, as Arjuna did: "Now I am your disciple, and a soul surrendered unto You. Please instruct me." (Bg. 2.7)

Bali Mahārāja surrendered everything to Kṛṣṇa. Then when there was nothing left, still Kṛṣṇa was asking for more. Bali said, "Please, therefore, place Your third lotus footstep on my head." (*Bhāg.* 8.22.2)

Bhaktivinoda Ṭhākura surrendered his body, his mind, his family, his home; he said he would live simply as an attendant for all these properties of Kṛṣṇa. (*Śaraṇāgati*)

Surrender means to give everything to Kṛṣṇa with no consideration of reward (*Śikṣāṣṭaka* #8).

To surrender wealth and other possessions doesn't mean to reject them but, rather, to live in Kṛṣṇa consciousness and use everything in the Lord's service (Rūpa Gosvāmī).

The greatest surrender of all was that of the gopīs, who risked social ruin and the dangers of the forest at night, and who gave Kṛṣṇa all their love and affection. They gave Kṛṣṇa their minds and always thought of Him, even after He had left Vṛndāvana. (*Kṛṣṇa,* Vol. I, "Kṛṣṇa's Hiding from the Gopīs.")

Surrender to the guru is unconditional. "My Guru Mahārāja gave me a task, and always I was discouraged by my godbrothers. But I did not forget him even for a moment, and I was determined to follow my duty." (Letter to Satsvarūpa, Nov. 5, 1972)

Kṛṣṇa rewards us according to our surrender to Him (Bg. 4.11).

One who knows how to surrender unto the Supreme Person attains the eternal kingdom. (Bg. 15.5)

Surrender means to rise early, bathe, and go to *maṅgala-ārati*, even when you lack spontaneous love to do so. *(Bhakti-rasāmṛta-sindhu)*

Surrender is to follow all the rules, even the small ones. (Śrīla Prabhupāda)

Sārvabhauma Bhaṭṭācārya describes that Lord Caitanya came to teach renunciation, knowledge of Himself, and the science of surrender, *bhakti-yoga*. Chanting Hare Kṛṣṇa is to surrender the speaking, the hearing, and the mind in the *yajña* of the holy name. Lord Caitanya taught that we should avoid the ten offenses in chanting and dedicate our lives to the instructions of the spiritual master. Surrender is not whimsical but authorized and scientific. If we practice, we will learn how to surrender. A devotee engaged in a life of full surrender to Kṛṣṇa has many things to do and does not waste a moment. His goal is to completely surrender to Kṛṣṇa so that he can be rid of all material desires and serve Kṛṣṇa more and more in the footsteps of the servant of the servant of the servant of the *gopīs*.

13

A devotee is desireless, *akāma*.

This quality should not be considered in a negative way, as if a devotee ultimately attains the state of nothingness, no desires. Devotional service means attaining fullness; it is sometimes compared to the waxing moon. On attaining full devotional service, therefore, a devotee finds that all his desires have become satisfied by his complete engagement in Kṛṣṇa consciousness. It is impossible to exist without any desire. Desire is a symptom of the living being.

As we have already explained, the real self is eternal, spiritual; the soul does not die when the body dies. To live means to desire *something*. The attempt of the impersonalist and voidist meditators to completely negate desires is futile. The soul, being part and parcel of the Supreme Whole, has the natural function to desire. By using high-sounding words of self-annihilation, or by a temporary suspension of desires, the impersonalist only deludes himself that he has escaped all ego and desire. Ultimately, he has to come away from his artificial position, either to again take up material life in the cycle of birth and death or, if he chooses, to take up pure loving service to Kṛṣṇa.

The real goal of desirelessness is revealed in the literal meaning of *akāma,* "without lust" Two words we should consider here are *kāma* and *prema*. *Kāma* means lust, or material desire, and *prema* means love. When a man loves a woman, his family, his country, or his vocational or intellectual pursuits, his "love" is really *kāma*, "lust," not *prema*, love. Love is reserved for Kṛṣṇa. Affections and attachments for things other than Kṛṣṇa are always some kind of *kāma*. Even desires to become one with the impersonal spirit are for one's own satisfaction and are *kāma*. *Śrīmad-Bhāgavatam* lists the various kinds of *kāmas*, or material desires, and the corresponding material worship one should undertake to fulfill those desires:

> One who desires to be absorbed in the impersonal brahmajyoti effulgence should worship the master of the Vedas . . . one who desires powerful sex should worship the heavenly king, Indra, and one who desires good progeny should worship the great progenitors called the Prajāpatīs. One who desires good fortune should worship Durgādevī, the superintendent of the material world. One desiring to be very powerful should worship fire, and one who aspires only after money should worship the Vasus . . .
>
> —*Bhāg*. 2.32–7

The list goes on and on, and each goal is identified by the word *kāma*. To fulfill such desires is the pursuit of the less intelligent. (Bg. 7.23) The intelligence of such worshipers has been bewildered by *māyā*, because no material goal can free anyone from birth and death or bring satisfaction of the self.

Only when one attains *prema*, love of Kṛṣṇa, can he come to the platform of desirelessness. Desiring only to please Kṛṣṇa is *akāma*. In pursuing the pure desire to serve Kṛṣṇa, one must be very steadfast. Material desires have been haunting every conditioned soul for many,

many lifetimes, and it is not easy for one to suddenly renounce them. Lord Kṛṣṇa advises that *kāma* cannot be given up artificially:

viṣayā vinivartante
nirāhārasya dehinaḥ
rasa-varjaṁ raso 'py asya
paraṁ dṛṣṭvā nivartate

> The embodied soul may be restricted from sense enjoyment, though the taste for sense objects remains. But, ceasing such engagements by experiencing a higher taste, he is fixed in consciousness.
>
> —Bg. 2.59

If one sincerely follows the process of Kṛṣṇa consciousness under the guidance of guru, *śāstra,* and *sādhu,* he will experience the higher taste and give up material desires even while still in the neophyte stage of devotional service. This may seem like a bold claim, but it is true; even a new devotee engaged in chanting, hearing, and serving finds sinful activities, like meat-eating, unthinkable. He satisfies his desires for palatable food by taking only food offered to Kṛṣṇa. He soon comes to regard intoxication as an unnecessary contamination; his life becomes so fulfilled in transcendental consciousness that he finds no need to depend on chemical stimulants. And he gives up illicit sex in favor of devotional service to Rādhā and Kṛṣṇa. Critics cannot understand the higher taste of Kṛṣṇa consciousness, nor can they experience it. If a person tries to assess the taste of honey in a bottle by looking at it or by licking the outside of the bottle, he will not be able to appreciate the taste. One has to open the bottle and dip inside. If one sincerely enters devotional service by chanting and hearing about the glories of the Lord, even one drop of that transcendental knowledge and transcendental pleasure will sustain him from degrading himself into sinful life.

In *The Nectar of Devotion,* Rūpa Gosvāmī cites three kinds of happiness: (1) happiness derived from material enjoyment, (2) happiness derived by identifying oneself with the Supreme Brahman, and (3) happiness derived from Kṛṣṇa consciousness. The supremacy of happiness derived from Kṛṣṇa consciousness is declared throughout the *śāstras*:

> My dear Lord, I repeatedly pray unto Your lotus feet that I may be stronger in devotional service. I simply pray that my Kṛṣṇa consciousness may be more strong and steady, because happiness derived out of Kṛṣṇa consciousness and devotional service is so powerful that with it one can have all the other perfections of religiousness, economic development, sense gratification and even the attainment of liberation from material existence.
>
> —*Hari-bhakti-sudhodaya*

Admittedly, until a devotee reaches unalloyed devotional service, he will still sometimes consider the possibility of becoming happy by material desires. Narottama dāsa Ṭhākura compares liberation (*mukti*) and material sense enjoyment (*bhukti*) to two witches who haunt the conditioned soul. In another song, Narottama compares *jñāna* (desire for non-devotional, philosophical knowledge) and *karma* (desire for material gains by work) to "two pots of poison."

How does a devotee persist in resisting material desires even before he has fully experienced the highest taste of spontaneous Kṛṣṇa consciousness? The answer is *tapāsya,* austerity. Atheistic psychologists abhor this idea of self-restraint, although they do not understand at all what it is. They advocate complete freedom, although the idea of freedom in relation to the body is ludicrous. Our body is forced to obey many natural laws, and if we impose upon our bodily activities moral principles of God consciousness, that is not unnatural, at least not for a human being. The principle of enforcing self-restraint to achieve a higher goal of happiness is something everyone does even for their ordinary material goals. A patient, for example, agrees to follow the instructions of a doctor, who may tell him he cannot travel nor eat certain foods he likes. The doctor is not repressing the normal personality of the patient. Rather, the patient, by following the doctor's restrictions, can regain his normal state of enjoyment. Ultimately, our normal state is spiritual; we are meant to live eternally in bliss and knowledge. But in the diseased state, we think we are this body.

There are two kinds of happiness: *preyaḥ,* immediate, and *śreyaḥ,* ultimate. A mature human being will forego *preyaḥ* to achieve *śreyaḥ.* Children, for example, want to play all day; if it were up to them, they would never go to school for education. Yet a young adult at college sometimes foregoes the immediate pleasure of socializing in the evening to study and advance his education. Austerity is like that. We are conditioned to perform acts contrary to Kṛṣṇa consciousness, and yet once we gain even a little knowledge from the *śāstra,* we know that human life is meant for more than mere animalistic satisfaction. Using our good intelligence, therefore, we control the mind and senses to reach the higher goal. Austerity is required to reach a purified state of consciousness, which is, in turn, required to reach transcendental happiness. Unless we can give up sense gratification and serve Kṛṣṇa, we cannot become free.

But even when we are still in the conditioned stage, *Śrīmad-Bhāgavatam* advises us to take to devotional service:

akāmaḥ sarva-kāmo vā
mokṣa-kāma udāra-dhīḥ
tīvreṇa bhakti-yogena
yajeta puruṣaṁ param

A person who has broader intelligence, whether he be full of material desire, without any material desire, or desiring liberation, must by all means worship the supreme whole, the Personality of Godhead.
—*Bhāg*. 2.3.10

A similar verse from the Second Canto of the *Śrīmad-Bhāgavatam* 2.1.11—*etan nirvidyamānānam*—states that even if one has material desires or desires for liberation, by chanting the holy name of Kṛṣṇa, he will come to the higher stage. Lord Caitanya also assures us in His *Śikṣāṣṭaka* that the chanting of Hare Kṛṣṇa will increase the ocean of transcendental bliss and give us a taste of the transcendental nectar for which we are always anxious. Rūpa Gosvāmī describes that the beginning devotee progresses through regular stages: faith, association with devotees, initiation by the spiritual master, giving up bad habits, steadiness, and finally, *ruci,* or taste. The sincere devotee comes to this stage progressively and automatically. After *ruci,* he goes on to the higher ecstasy and attachment of *bhāva* and *prema.*

A devotee, therefore, does not begrudge austerity; he willingly struggles to overcome his lower nature. Nothing valuable is achieved without endeavor, and Kṛṣṇa consciousness is the most valuable thing. The devotee receives immense help from the spiritual master and from Kṛṣṇa in the heart. Kṛṣṇa promises, "To those who are constantly devoted to serving Me with love, I give the understanding by which they can come to Me." (Bg. 10.10)

The Lord also sometimes helps the reluctant devotee by force. If a devotee is sincerely desirous of attaining love of God and yet at the same time has strong material desires, Lord Kṛṣṇa sometimes intervenes.

yasyāham anugṛhṇāmi
hariṣye tad-dhanaà śanaiḥ
tato 'dhanaṁ tyajanty asya
svajanā duḥkha-duḥkhitam

> If I especially favor someone, I gradually deprive him of his wealth. Then the relatives and friends of such a poverty-stricken man abandon him. In this way he suffers one distress after another.
>
> —*Bhāg.* 10.88.8

Two levels of advancement in devotional service are *sādhana bhakti,* following the rules and regulations out of obligation to the spiritual master, and *rāgānugā-bhakti,* the advanced stage of spontaneous loving service to Kṛṣṇa. It is important to note that all stages, even the beginning, are included within *bhakti*. Bhakti can be compared to the mango, which in the early stage is green but when mature is ripe and delicious. But the mango, even when unripe, is still a mango. Similarly, all *bhakti* is absolute, and under the guidance of a pure devotee, even the beginner can engage in pure devotional service. If an iron rod is kept steadily in the blazing fire, the rod will eventually become warmer and warmer until it becomes red hot. Then it will act as fire. Similarly, any person who takes to the authorized process of devotional service will gradually throw off his false identity and see himself as the eternal servant of Kṛṣṇa. Even in his probationary period, a devotee's application of his senses and mind in Kṛṣṇa's service saves him from material desires.

No one should criticize a neophyte devotee who, although not yet fully free from the witches of *bhukti* and *mukti,* is sincerely struggling against such desires and trying to come to the platform of full Kṛṣṇa consciousness. Because he is earnestly trying to serve Kṛṣṇa, he is better than the most accomplished nondevotional philosopher or speculator. He is performing the real function of human life, and thus he is already victorious. Rūpa Gosvāmī says the price for pure love of Kṛṣṇa is intense desire. It will therefore take time and effort. But success is guaranteed for the sincere practitioner, and whatever he does is his permanent gain.

14
A devotee is indifferent to material acquisitions, *anīha*.

Sometimes a specific quality of the Vaiṣṇava will come forth and shine, just as at night a certain star may first appear and then others. On another occasion, another quality may be called for and come forth. And sometimes, like blossoms on a tree in spring, many show at once. The pure devotee is capable of showing one quality after another, not as a theatrical performance but *as is needed* in the course of rendering service to Kṛṣṇa and the Vaiṣṇavas. And all the transcendental qualities come naturally to him, without separate effort, as integral parts of his Kṛṣṇa consciousness.

We should not demand a consistency according to material standards in a devotee's display of these qualities. His meekness does not mean he cannot on occasion become angry. Detachment does not mean he cannot use material things in the service of Kṛṣṇa. The devotee *is* consistent, but not in a small-minded way. All a devotee's actions are consistent with his rendering pure, unalloyed devotional service to Kṛṣṇa.

The quality of *anīha,* indifference to material acquisitions, is another part of the Vaiṣṇava's opulence. He doesn't have to acquire things because he is already satisfied in devotional service. A devotee may use material things in the service of Kṛṣṇa, but he doesn't become attached or dependent on them. He may serve Kṛṣṇa with millions of dollars, construct buildings, and profusely publish Kṛṣṇa conscious literatures; but even if he has nothing material to use, he can serve Kṛṣṇa just by chanting Hare Kṛṣṇa.

This quality is well-illustrated in the story of the oldest man. There was once a sage who was so old his years could hardly be calculated. He was supposed to live until all the hairs on his body fell out, but only one hair would fall out during one lifetime of Brahmā (311 trillion, 40 billion years). The sage was very hairy, so his life span was incalculable. One day the sage's disciples approached him, desiring to build him a shelter. "Master," they said, "you have no shelter from the sun or rain as you chant Hare Kṛṣṇa here on the bank of the Ganges. May we please build you a simple cottage?" The sage replied, "No. This life is temporary."

The temporality of life in this material world makes the devotee-transcendentalist neglectful about acquiring "possessions" that he will sooner or later have to leave behind. So this is the basis for his indifference to material acquisitions. The very word *material* implies temporality. And ultimately, material things are lost at death. But *kāma,* the desire for getting and keeping things, will cause a person to suffer birth after birth.

The devotee is indifferent to the triumph of winning some post or prize, nor does he like to go out and buy things for himself (although he loves to shop for Kṛṣṇa's service). He doesn't want a wife, a trophy, or a post. He doesn't want to put the stuffed head of an animal on his wall or keep extra clothes or ornaments or special foods. He remains materially poor with his heart clear of all material acquisitions, even though he uses many things in the service of the Lord. The world emperor Mahārāja Parīkṣit, although surrounded by great opulence, remained unaffected because he used everything in the service of the Lord. But when he received seven days' notice of his death, he thought it better to leave all his royal paraphernalia and sit by the Ganges without eating or drinking, while hearing *Śrīmad-Bhāgavatam* from Śukadeva Gosvāmī.

A devotee must be firmly situated in the realization of his spiritual identity, *ahaṁ brahmāsmi*. He knows he is not this body, and he experiences the satisfaction of the spirit soul—*brahma-bhūtaḥ prasannātma*. Being firmly situated in the higher taste of Kṛṣṇa consciousness, the devotee's quality of *anīha* flourishes. He does not become attracted to material things, even though for preaching purposes he may have to associate with women and money, the most dangerous material allurements. Once someone asked Śrīla Prabhupāda whether, since he was a swami, he could stab a knife into his hand without feeling pain. Such a feat, Śrīla Prabhupāda replied, was not perfection; in fact, it could be done just by taking an anesthetic. He said swami actually meant that one can be in the presence of beautiful women yet be unaffected by them.

A devotee does the compassionate work of staying within materialistic society, rather than hiding in seclusion to save himself; he moves amid material attractions and disturbances. He therefore must have the quality of *anīha*. The devotee practices *anīha* bravely and sometimes approaches persons who are fully absorbed in material life. Sometimes he sits with the *karmī* and tells him of Kṛṣṇa consciousness, and sometimes he is offered material attractions and material troubles. But he remains always *anīha* and also draws the sense-gratifier away from material acquisition.

All glories to the peaceful Vaiṣṇavas situated in *anīha,* who are delivering the entire world. How wonderfully Kṛṣṇa has blessed His pure devotees. The more we describe their qualities, the more we can see the Vaiṣṇavas' qualities are there for the benefit of others. The devotees live among us to teach us to free ourselves from unwanted things and become attracted to the lotus feet of Kṛṣṇa, where the pure devotees themselves are firmly situated.

15

A devotee is fixed, *sthira.*

The Vaiṣṇava qualities may not appear as soon as a person takes to devotional service, but gradually they will develop as the devotee matures. *Nitya-siddha* devotees, those who never fall to the conditioned state, have all the Vaiṣṇava qualities eternally. But when a conditioned soul comes to Kṛṣṇa consciousness, he must serve patiently, and in time all the twenty-six qualities will develop. The qualities of a devotee, because they are the very nature of the soul, are within each person, and they become manifest through the process of *bhakti.* As a match contains fire, as milk contains butter, and as a dull knife contains within it a sharp blade, and as the proper process—striking the match, churning the milk, whetting the dull blade—brings out the inherent quality, so *bhakti-yoga* brings out the qualities of the Vaiṣṇava. Love of God and the twenty-six concomitant qualities of a devotee are within each of us.

Rūpa Gosvāmī describes the devotee's gradual progress. A conditioned soul has to first hear about Kṛṣṇa with faith (*śraddhā*). Then he associates with devotees (*sādhu-saṅga*). Next he takes initiation from a bona fide spiritual master (*bhajana-kriyā*). And as he follows the rules and regulations of devotional service under the spiritual master's order, he loses his bad habits (*anartha-nivṛtti*). The next step is steadiness, *niṣṭha,* and this is a close synonym to *sthira,* or fixed. A devotee must be fixed in the Absolute Truth.

If someone challenges a fixed devotee with atheistic or impersonalistic philosophy, the devotee cannot be shaken. He considers all conclusions other than Kṛṣṇa consciousness to be nonsense. He won't change his philosophy next year and come up with a new theory of truth. In *Śrīmad-Bhāgavatam* Nārada Muni contrasts the steadiness of the devotee with the fickleness of the *karmī*:

> Mixed with the mode of passion, the unsteady intelligence of every living entity is like a prostitute who changes dresses just to attract one's attention. If one fully engages in temporary fruitive activities, not understanding how this is taking place, what does he actually gain?
>
> PURPORT
>
> Karmīs change their professions at any moment, but a Kṛṣṇa conscious person does not change his profession, for his only profession is to attract the attention of Kṛṣṇa by chanting the Hare Kṛṣṇa mantra and living a very simply life, without following daily changes of fashion. In our Kṛṣṇa consciousness movement, fashionable persons are taught to adopt one fashion—the dress of a Vaiṣṇava with a shaved head and *tilaka*. They are taught to be always clean in mind, dress and eating in order to be fixed in Kṛṣṇa consciousness. What is the use of changing one's dress, sometimes wearing long hair and a long beard and sometimes dressing otherwise? This is not good. One should not waste his time in such frivolous activities. One should always be fixed in Kṛṣṇa consciousness and take the cure of devotional service with firm determination.
>
> —*Bhāg*. 6.5.14

An unsteady neophyte devotee, although able to prosecute devotional practices under favorable circumstances, deviates in the face of strong allurements. The Vedic histories tell of meditating sages distracted by beautiful women. And a devotee also, in the neophyte stage, may fall victim to the attraction of the opposite sex. Or a situation of distress may unfix a weaker devotee. Often devotees are harassed and their preaching disrupted by the non-devotees. If a devotee is fixed, however, he will not abandon chanting Hare Kṛṣṇa, even at the cost of his life. Sometimes devotees quarrel among themselves, and this is another discouragement that might sway a weak devotee from following his spiritual master's order.

Firm faith in the spiritual master is paramount. Viśvanātha Cakravartī instructs us in his *Gurv-aṣṭakam* that to please the guru is to please Kṛṣṇa, whereas to displease the guru is to lose one's standing in spiritual life. One who displeases the spiritual master loses his fixed course and wanders aimlessly like a ship without a rudder. Without firm faith in the spiritual master, one cannot be *sthira*. Prahlāda Mahārāja, considering his debt to his spiritual master, says, "I was falling into the ways of the common man, and my spiritual master Nārada saved me. How could I ever leave him?"

A devotee is fixed in the philosophy of the Absolute Truth, not only intellectually but out of love. And as the devotee is fixed on Kṛṣṇa and no one else, so is Kṛṣṇa fixed on His devotee: "The pure devotee is always within the core of My heart, and I am always in the heart of the pure devotee. My devotees do not know anything else but Me, and I do not know anyone else but them." (*Bhāg*. 9.4.68) Kṛṣṇa is so fixed in His relationship with His devotees that He never leaves Vṛndāvana, but remains always engaged there in pastimes with His eternal associates.

How can a devotee become fixed in this position? *Kecit kevalayā bhaktyā*: by practicing devotional service. We should proceed scrupulously in our chanting and hearing and serving the order of the spiritual master as our life's duty. Certainly being fixed will come about in this way, by regular practice. As a devotee continues hearing, whatever conviction he lacks will come to him as a gradual realization. When a neophyte devotee chants Hare Kṛṣṇa, he does not taste the full happiness of chanting the holy names. But as he continues, the original sweetness of the holy name will manifest. The advanced chanter is fixed in repeating the holy name just like a bee is fixed in the honey of the flower—nothing can take him out. Determined practice will bring the desired result; by proper *sādhana* one will become fixed. This applies not only to gaining the quality of *sthira* but to all other qualities as well. Chanting and hearing will produce truthfulness, mercifulness, cleanliness, surrender to Kṛṣṇa, indifference to material acquisitions, and so on. As *Śrīmad-Bhāgavatam* explains, " . . . all that is troublesome to the heart is almost completely destroyed, and loving service unto the Personality of Godhead, who is praised with transcendental songs, is established as an irrevocable fact." (*Bhāg*. 1.2.18)

16

A devotee completely controls the six bad qualities, *vijita-ṣaḍ-guṇa.*

In the material world the spirit soul always has the tendency to fall under the control of *māyā.* Although it is impossible for the Supreme Personality of Godhead to come under the control of His own *māyā,* the *jīvas,* being marginal, come sometimes under the material energy and sometimes under the spiritual energy. The pure devotees, although marginal energies, stay always under the shelter of the internal energy; thus they never succumb to the bad qualities. As *Bhagavad-gītā* 2.70 states: "A person who is not disturbed by the incessant flow of desires—that enter like rivers into the ocean, which is ever being filled but is always still—can alone achieve peace, and not the man who strives to satisfy such desires."

The six bad qualities are lust (*kāma*), anger (*krodha*), greed (*lobha*), illusion (*moha*), madness (*mada*), and envy (*matsarya*). A pure devotee controls these qualities by full engagement in the service of Kṛṣṇa. Although the six bad qualities are material, they can be used in Kṛṣṇa's service. This tranforms them. The bad qualities are perverted reflections of qualities existing in an original pure state in the spiritual world. Narottama dāsa Ṭhākura writes, *kāma kṛṣṇa-karmārpane*: "Lust can be transformed into love of Kṛṣṇa." In *Śrīmad-Bhāgavatam*

Nārada Muni informs King Yudhiṣṭhira how Lord Kṛṣṇa can be served by transforming material qualities into devotional service:

> My dear King Yudhiṣṭhira, the gopīs by their lusty desires, Kaṁsa by his fear, Śiśupāla and other kings by envy, the Yadus by their familial relationship with Kṛṣṇa, you Pāṇḍavas by your great affection for Kṛṣṇa, and we, the general devotees, by our devotional service, have obtained the mercy of Kṛṣṇa.
>
> —*Bhāg*. 7.1.31

Let us consider each of the six bad qualities and how the pure devotee controls them by engaging himself in the service of Kṛṣṇa.

1. Lust, *kāma*. Lust is epitomized by sex desire. The *gopīs* approached Kṛṣṇa as a beautiful young boy, and yet we know this is the complete opposite of mundane lust. We have been warned not to imitate the *gopīs*. So how can we, who are trying to practice pure devotional service, understand lust in service to Kṛṣṇa? *Bhagavad-gītā* 7.11 states, *dharmāviruddho bhūteṣu kāmo 'smi:* "I am sex life which is not contrary to religious principles." When *kāma* is controlled, it is not illicit and can be used in Kṛṣṇa's service. In the beginning there may be material desires, but when sex is regulated and used for the service of the Lord, it is transcendental. Prabhodhānanda Sarasvatī gives the example of a snake with its poisoned fangs removed. Just the sight of a poisonous snake causes great fear, but if the snake's fangs have been removed, then the snake is no longer frightening. Similarly, the uncontrolled senses have been compared to poisonous serpents, which bite without provocation. But sinfulness in sensual activity is eradicated when the devotee uses his body as an instrument for Kṛṣṇa.

Aside from the *gopīs*, Kubjā also approached Kṛṣṇa with lusty feelings. She wanted to serve Kṛṣṇa by offering Him her body. But as soon as Kṛṣṇa's lotus feet touched her, her lusty contamination vanished. Similarly, the aborigine women living in the forest of Vṛndāvana approached Kṛṣṇa from a distance. *Śrīmad-Bhāgavatam* describes them as being so lusty that even their own lovers' touching their breasts could not satisfy their lust. But when they saw on the ground the *kuṅkuma* marks from Kṛṣṇa's lotus feet, they smeared that dust on their breasts and felt all their lust relieved. These feelings are surely transcendental, because mundane lust can never be satisfied.

In *Bhagavad-gītā* 3.37, Arjuna asks by what one is impelled to sinful acts, even unwillingly. Kṛṣṇa replies, "It is lust only, Arjuna, which is born of contact with the material modes of passion and later transformed into wrath, and which is the all-devouring sinful enemy of this world."

Lust is the spirit soul's original love for Kṛṣṇa after becoming contaminated by association with the mode of passion. Just as milk touched by sour tamarind becomes yogurt, so *prema* (love of God) becomes "soured" into *kāma*. When the *jīvas* wrongly desire their own sense enjoyment, Kṛṣṇa allows them to come to this material world and take on different material bodies. But lust can never satisfy the *jīva* soul. Only when he transfers his desire back to the service of Kṛṣṇa can he experience eternal bliss. Even while in the material world, if by the grace of the spiritual master and the Vaiṣṇavas a *jīva* establishes his relationship with Kṛṣṇa, he can revive his pure desire. Once the *jīva* takes up devotional service under the direction of the spiritual master, his lust is turned into love. The pure presence of Kṛṣṇa removes all impurities. Devotional service can be compared to the sun. The sun is so powerful that when it shines on something impure—like a puddle of urine—it sterilizes the impure place.

I have given examples of persons purified by contacting Kṛṣṇa during His *līlā* on this earth, but how can we expect the good fortune of losing our lust in that way? The answer is that we can also enter Kṛṣṇa's *līlā* by hearing from authorized sources. To hear of Him in an unauthorized way, however, can result in *prākṛta-sahajiyā. Prākṛta-sahajiyā* is a perverted form of Vaiṣṇavism in which the practitioner tries to approach Kṛṣṇa while still engaging in mundane sex. But when *kṛṣṇa-līlā* is heard properly from the right source, it removes mundane lust and arouses the spiritual desire to hear more and more about Kṛṣṇa. Hearing about Kṛṣṇa's pastimes with the *gopīs* in the *rāsa* dance is a specific remedy for lust. By engaging in Deity worship in the temple, a devotee can also directly approach Rādhā-Kṛṣṇa on the order of the spiritual master.

2. Anger, *krodha*. Lust can never be satisfied, and therefore it is followed by anger. Anger follows lust like a younger brother. When a person falls into uncontrolled anger, he can kill even his best friend or dear relative. When anger spreads, the whole body becomes polluted. But anger can also be used in the service of Kṛṣṇa, by directing it against the enemies of Kṛṣṇa.

The famous example is Hanumān, Lord Rāma's warrior-servitor who fought against the forces of Rāvana. Lord Caitanya also showed transcendental anger when He heard that Jagāi and Mādhāi had assaulted Lord Nityānanda.

Devotional anger may therefore take on the form of fighting. The *kṣatriya* devotee cannot tolerate seeing the

Lord's devotee or innocent persons or creatures hurt. Mahārāja Parīkṣit thus became angry at the sight of a *śūdra* beating a cow. Arjuna was not angry and, therefore, could not fight on the Battlefield of Kurukṣetra. Kṛṣṇa, by His preaching, incited Arjuna to fight in transcendental anger. A devotee may also direct anger against bogus gurus and other misleaders of the people. When a devotee hears bad propaganda against devotional service, he may write articles against the demons or actively preach in another way.

Uninformed Hindus sometimes think that a *sādhu* can never show anger. Such persons do not understand transcendental anger. Of course, anger should not be uncontrolled or used to combat an insult toward oneself.

Once a snake, after meeting Nārada Muni, became very peaceful. But when the local village boys learned of the snake's nonviolence, they began throwing stones at him. When the snake complained to Nārada that his nonviolence had brought on these attacks, Nārada advised the snake to remain peaceful but to raise up, show his hood, and scare the boys away. This is an example of using controlled anger.

Anger should be controlled and used only in the service of the Lord. Sometimes a teacher will assume an angry face or gesture to instruct a student. He teaches by kind words, encouragement, and also occasionally by chastisement and show of anger. But this anger is controlled; anger can only be used as an instrument in devotional service.

Anger is also manifested in a very advanced stage of devotional service as a kind of ecstatic attachment toward Kṛṣṇa; many examples of this are in *The Nectar of Devotion.* Once when Kṛṣṇa and His friends returned from the forests of Vṛndāvana, the cowherd boys reported to mother Yaśodā that Kṛṣṇa had gone alone into the Tālavana forest and killed Dhenukāsura. When mother Yaśodā heard how the boys had requested Kṛṣṇa to go on such a dangerous mission alone, she became perturbed and looked upon the boys with anger. On another occasion, when at the assembly of Rājasuya the demon Śiśupala insulted Kṛṣṇa, Kṛṣṇa's cousin Nakula spoke with great anger: "If Kṛṣṇa is derided by anyone, I declare herewith as a Pāṇḍava that I will kick his helmet with my left foot, and I will strike him with my arrows, which are as good as *yama-daṇḍa,* the scepter of Yamarāja!"

3. Greed, *lobha.* A greedy person wants to accumulate as much as possible for himself—much more than he actually needs. Obsessed with taking for himself, he conflicts with others and has no mercy for them. Out of greed one nation allows millions of people in other parts of the world to starve. The greedy people of one nation take many times over their requirements for food and fuel, while others go without. So greed can become a great evil. But because a devotee is greedy to use everything for the Supreme Personality of Godhead's satisfaction, his greed benefits everyone.

A devotee wants the whole world at Kṛṣṇa's lotus feet. He wants not just himself but all the fallen souls to take shelter under the instructions of his spiritual master. He wants as many people as possible to gather before the Deity of Kṛṣṇa, and he is not satisfied as long as many people are still not surrendered to Kṛṣṇa. There is a saying that if you give a Vaiṣṇava a million dollars, he will be at your door the next day. And when you ask him, "Sir, why are you back? I just gave you a million dollars yesterday" he will reply, "Yes, and thank you very much. But I have already spent it in the service of Kṛṣṇa. Can you please give more?"

A pure devotee can spend any amount of money for Kṛṣṇa. Kṛṣṇa is unlimited, and consequently, an unlimited number of books can be published, an unlimited number of temples can be opened, and all civic activities can be engaged in the glorification of the Supreme Personality of Godhead. To meditate in this way on how everything can be used to serve Kṛṣṇa is a kind of greed, but this greed is transcendental and beneficial for all the whole world. The desire to see everyone in the universe saved from hellish suffering is not a material emotion.

For himself, the devotee can never get enough service. Twenty-four hours a day is not enough time for serving Kṛṣṇa. A devotee wants to keep reading about Kṛṣṇa more and more, and he wants to keep preaching. He doesn't want to greedily monopolize devotional service; rather, he understands that devotional service is unlimited. He wants to see others take it, and he also wants to take more and more. In his ambitious desire to serve Kṛṣṇa, a devotee sometimes goes without sleeping or eating.

This transcendental greed for performing service to Kṛṣṇa culminates in *laulyam,* the intense hankering to serve Kṛṣṇa. Śrīla Prabhupāda writes in *The Nectar of Devotion* that a devotee should want to serve Kṛṣṇa so badly he cries for it. When one is absorbed in intense hankering for service, no possibility of material greed arises.

4. Illusion, *moha*. The main illusion of the conditioned soul is that he thinks of his body as the self and the material world as his home. This illusion will kill him, just as an animal in the desert is killed running after a mirage of water. A person who does not know Kṛṣṇa, who thinks that he himself is the absolute, is in complete illusion, and his human life is therefore doomed. But

when one comes to the stage of faithfully hearing about Kṛṣṇa, understanding that Kṛṣṇa is the Supreme and that all living entities are His infinitesimal parts and parcels, how can there be illusion? A devotee who has a bona fide spiritual master should know and be free of misconception. When Arjuna became enlightened by Kṛṣṇa's teachings in *Bhagavad-gītā,* he declared, *naṣṭo mohaḥ*: "My illusion is now gone."

But there is a transcendental illusion known as *yoga-māyā*. By *yoga-māyā* a liberated devotee can think he has become the father or mother of Kṛṣṇa. Kṛṣṇa does not need a protector, and yet He accepts mother Yaśodā as His protector and chastiser. When Kṛṣṇa, as a child, fell into the River Yamunā, His father, Vasudeva, was in the illusion of extreme anxiety over Kṛṣṇa. Actually, Kṛṣṇa could not drown in the river, but as an expression of love for Kṛṣṇa, Vasudeva became mad with anxiety. Kṛṣṇa's falling into the water was His arrangement to intensify the paternal feelings of His devotee. Kṛṣṇa is so attached to His pure devotees, the *gopīs,* that He can never forget them or reject them, yet in their conjugal exchange He allows them to act like rejected lovers, just to increase their sublime sense of separation from Him. These exchanges of *yoga-māyā* are not really delusions, but are confidential pastimes between the Supreme Lord and His eternal associates. They are ultimate reality, but they are not manifest to the general devotees.

5. Madness, *mada*. When a person contemplates the sense objects, he develops desire; he then becomes angry; this leads to delusion and bewilderment of memory. In extreme cases of madness a person cannot even perform bodily functions, and he becomes like a vegetable or a wild beast. But all conditioned souls, even those passing as sane, are more or less crazy. As described in *Śrīmad-Bhāgavatam*:

nūnaṁ pramattaḥ kurute vikarma
yad indriya-prītaya āpṛṇoti
na sādhu manye yata ātmano 'yam
asann api kleśada āsa dehaḥ

When a person considers sense gratification the aim of life, he certainly becomes mad after materialistic living and engages in all kinds of sinful activity. He does not know that due to his past misdeeds he has already received a body which, although temporary, is the cause of his misery. Actually the living entity should not have taken on a material body, but he has been awarded the material body for sense gratification. Therefore, I think it is not befitting an intelligent man to involve himself again in the activities of sense gratification by which he perpetually gets material bodies one after another.

—*Bhāg*. 5.5.4

The above verse, spoken by Lord Ṁṣabhadeva, describes madness as being impelled by sense gratification. Because of their uncontrolled senses, people are willing to slaughter the cow and to kill the child in the womb. This killing is also done during wartime in the madness of nationalism. Because of their mad acts for sense gratification, people have to transmigrate, body after body. For a person to accept his body as the self is crazy, because at the time of death everything he lived for will vanish.

6. Envy, *matsarya*. According to Cāṇakya Paṇḍita, nothing is worse than an envious man. A snake is considered a very envious creature because he attacks other animals without reason. But the snake can be charmed by the snake charmer, whereas nothing can control an envious man. An envious person is unhappy

to see others' good fortune, and he is happy to see others' failure. But when one takes to devotional service, he loses this poisonous mentality; he becomes humble and wants to serve Kṛṣṇa.

Sometimes among devotees there is a spirit of competition, but ultimately they are mutual well-wishers and are not disturbing to Kṛṣṇa. Śrīla Prabhupāda has therefore said that in the spiritual world there is no envy. Śiśupāla approached Kṛṣṇa in envy, but his contact with Kṛṣṇa purified him. We are not advised, however, to try to become liberated by being envious of Kṛṣṇa. Śrīla Prabhupāda explains that the demons' liberation is not the highest:

> Kaṁsa and other enemies of Kṛṣṇa merged into the existence of Brahman, but why should Kṛṣṇa's friends and devotees have the same position? Kṛṣṇa's devotees attain the association of the Lord as His constant companions, either in Vṛndāvana or in the Vaikuṇṭha planets.
>
> —*Bhāg.* 7.1.31, purport

Although I have described how a devotee can control the six bad qualities by engaging them in the service of Kṛṣṇa, another question may still persist: "What does a devotee do if he feels the urge for the bad quality in its material form?" When this happens we must use self-control. When Bhṛgu purposely neglected honoring Lord Brahmā to test if he would become angry, Lord Brahmā did become angry, but almost immediately thereafter he controlled his anger by his intelligence. Kṛṣṇa also advises that while practicing yoga, one has to constantly bring the wandering mind back under the control of the higher self. Being able to control the bad qualities is the criterion of *gosvāmī,* or a controller of the senses. A devotee has to gain the strength to rightly say "No!" to desires for material things.

The opposite of *gosvāmī* is *godāsa,* one who is the servant of his own senses. Whatever the tongue or genitals dictate, the *godāsa* obediently performs. But a *godāsa* cannot be a devotee. When Hiraṇyakaśipu asked his son, Prahlāda, to tell him how to become Kṛṣṇa conscious, Prahlāda replied that it was impossible. Hiraṇyakaśipu could not become a devotee because of his uncontrolled senses.

Control of the senses is possible not by dry restraint or mechanical repression but by transcendental knowledge (*jñāna*) and transcendental taste (vi*jñāna*).

17
A devotee eats only as much as required, *mita bhuk.*

If a person were to practice this quality only, out of the twenty-six qualities of a devotee, he would not become a pure Vaiṣṇava. So perhaps we may consider *mita bhuk* a minor quality. But, on the other hand, if a devotee was to somehow fail to practice *mita bhuk,* it could be a serious flaw. Therefore, this quality is not inconsequential, and so Lord Caitanya has included it in His list. *Bhagavad-gītā* 6.16 sets the standard of eating for the *bhakti-yogi*: "One should not eat too much or eat too little." What does it mean, to eat enough and not too much? It is an individual matter, according to the size of one's body. An individual can honestly sense when he has eaten sufficiently for strength and nourishment. Once I asked Śrīla Prabhupāda how much was the proper amount to eat, and he replied, "Eat what you can easily digest." He also quoted common sense maxims: "There are two mistakes one can make in eating. One is to eat too much, and the other is to eat too little. If one has to make a mistake, it is better to make the mistake of eating too little." Another maxim stated by Śrīla Prabhupāda: "A child cannot eat too much; an old man cannot eat too little."

According to the yoga of sense control, the tongue, belly, and genitals form a straight line, and all three can be controlled if the tongue is controlled. If the tongue is uncontrolled, then a person will eat too much. His stomach will be overloaded and will then put pressure upon his genitals, and the result will be great demand for sex.

A devotee always eats *kṛṣṇa-prasādam,* the remnants of the offerings to Kṛṣṇa. But still the rule of *mita bhuk* applies, as Śrīla Prabhupāda notes in *The Nectar of Instruction:*

> However, if one accepts *prasāda* only because of its palatable taste and thus eats too much, he also falls prey to trying to satisfy the demands of the tongue. Śrī Caitanya Mahāprabhu taught us to avoid very palatable dishes even while eating *prasāda*. If we offer palatable dishes to the Deity with the intention of eating such nice food, we are involved in trying to satisfy the demands of the tongue. If we accept the invitation of a rich man with the idea of receiving palatable food, we are also trying to satisfy the demands of the tongue.
>
> —*Upadeśāmṛta* #1, purport

One purpose in studying the qualities of the devotee is for guidance in devotional service. So the warnings about overeating *prasādam* are important and should be applied. If overeating produces indigestion, or excessive sleeping, or sexual agitation, then the devotee's obvious recourse is to decrease his eating. This is practical use of intelligence. A devotee should use his intelligence to overrule the urges of the senses and the mind. If I know my mind is asking me to do something wrong, then by the exercise of my intelligence, I should refrain. Proper intelligence can guide us when we are receiving dictation from the spiritual master and the Supersoul. We can therefore refrain from overeating—

out of austerity, and finally, out of ecstatic absorption in Kṛṣṇa consciousness.

An apparently contradictory description of the Vaiṣṇava's eating is related in *Caitanya-caritāmṛta.* Kṛṣṇadāsa Kavirāja repeatedly writes that Lord Caitanya would order His devotees to eat "up to the neck." Sometimes Lord Caitanya Mahāprabhu would serve large quantities of *prasādam* to the devotees with His own hand. In the *Caitanya-caritāmṛta,* the exchange of offering and receiving *prasādam* is obviously an important loving pastime between the Lord and His devotees. Sometimes the Lord's loving devotees would induce Him to eat large quantities of *prasādam.*

In coming to understand this phenomenon, an expression by Śrīla Prabhupāda is helpful: "In Kṛṣṇa consciousness, our feasting is fasting, and our fasting is feasting." In other words, a devotee, whether he eats or fasts, has the same goal: service to Kṛṣṇa. Certainly if Lord Caitanya or the spiritual master is personally serving *prasādam,* the devotee cannot stand upon the rules and regulations and refuse to eat. On the occasion of a Vaiṣṇava festival Kṛṣṇa's desire may sometimes be that the devotees eat "up to the neck" to satisfy the wishes of the Vaiṣṇava and the spiritual master. Such eating sometimes becomes a joyful, joking exchange and is transcendental to the rules and regulations. But in the normal daily course of life, the devotee should not be interested in eating big amounts. Raghunātha dāsa Gosvāmī is celebrated for serving a large feast to Lord Nityānanda and the Vaiṣṇavas at Panihati in Bengal. But Raghunātha dāsa Gosvāmī is also celebrated for minimizing his own intake of food to an extreme minimum. "Eat sumptuously," Śrīla Prabhupāda used to say, "but not too much."

18

A devotee is without inebriation, *apramatta.*

Apramattaḥ is the opposite of *pramattaḥ,* which means crazy. The materialist is crazy because he acts on the demands of the senses, forcing himself unnecessarily to continue his cycle of birth and death. But the devotee is *apramattaḥ,* sane. Śrīla Prabhupāda has translated *apramattaḥ* as "without inebriation," and this inebriation specifically refers to intoxication. A person intoxicated on alcohol, for example, has lost his balance and becomes sentimental, violent, or incoherent.

Sometimes, in the name of spiritual life, a person dresses whimsically and thinks he is Jesus Christ or another incarnation of God. With a far-off look in his eyes, he talks strangely and gives people the impression that he is crazy. Such a person may have some inkling that spiritual life is desirable, but without guidance he has fallen into illusion in the name of saintly life. But one who is truly on the devotional path under the guidance of guru, *śāstra,* and *sādhu* is sane. He wears the dress and paraphernalia of the Vaiṣṇava, which although strange to the uninformed, is highly orthodox. His habits are pure, his speech *paramparā*. He can deal sanely, and even diplomatically, with the *karmīs* and with the affairs of the material world.

The devotee's sanity, however, goes beyond the appearance of coolheaded poise. Understanding his position as the tiny part and parcel of the Lord, he does not have the insane view that he is the center of the universe or that life is meant for sense enjoyment. Nor is he insanely attached to family members. In *Śrīmad-Bhāgavatam* 2.1.4 Śukadeva Gosvāmī uses the word *pramattaḥ* to describe the householder who does not inquire into the problems of life: *teṣām pramatto nidhanam.* In that verse Śrīla Prabhupāda translates *pramattaḥ* as "too attached." The householder is so attached to his body, children, and wife that he neglects to inquire into the Absolute Truth. Śukadeva Gosvāmī says, "Although sufficiently experienced, they still do not see their inevitable destruction."

The nondevotee often sees the devotee as a crazy fellow. Mādhavendra Purī wrote that even though "the wealthy mammonites may point me out as mad," still he would take to Kṛṣṇa consciousness. Sometimes to make a full commitment to Kṛṣṇa consciousness, a devotee gives up a promising professional career, leaves aside a Ph.D., or gives up an attractive girlfriend, and, consequently, is thought of as crazy. Living the philosophy of "since ignorance is bliss, 'tis folly to be wise," the *karmīs* cannot see any good reason why the devotee has given up pursuing happiness in the material field. They think maybe he is psychologically incapable, an escapist, brainwashed perhaps, or maybe just a little crazy.

When the parents of one of Prabhupāda's disciples remarked they thought their son was crazy, Śrīla Prabhupāda wrote an essay entitled, "Who is Crazy?" He said the devotee thinks the nondevotee is crazy, and the *karmī* thinks the devotee is crazy. The question has to be settled by objective reasoning. I have already stated

Śrīla Prabhupāda's conclusion: he who lives and works for the perishable body is crazy, while he who invests his energy in that which is eternal is sane. In the age of Kali the whole world is crazy, and to be sane is to be thought mad. By the standard of the Absolute Truth, the devotee has attained the right balance between material duties and spiritual duties. Bhaktivinoda Ṭhākura has explained that both material duties and spiritual duties should run along parallel lines. But if the pursuance of the material duties seriously hampers the path of self-realization, then the material duties should be reduced.

A devotee is not inebriated. He is not lopsided. He is not intoxicated by material pleasure. He reduces his material needs to a simple level and patiently dedicates his life to the service of Kṛṣṇa. His life is therefore the real example of moderation, balance, and sanity.

19

A devotee is respectful, *mānada*.

The *Śikṣāṣṭaka* describes how the devotee offers respects to others without expecting any respect for himself. He is respectful even to the ant. Why? Because he sees all living beings as part and parcel of Kṛṣṇa. A materialist is not deeply respectful to others because his concern is to get respect for himself. But the devotee wants to be the servant, not the master, and taking that humble position, he respects the lives of others. He respects their right to live and doesn't want to hurt or disturb anyone. He respects that all living beings have been given their life by Kṛṣṇa, and he knows that he has no right to take it away. He sees all living beings equally and respects them equally.

The nondevotee, however, takes a critical view: "I don't think a devotee is so respectful. He doesn't respect the president of the United States or the demigods or family or motherhood or freedom in sexuality or culture, politics, tradition—anything! He makes a big thing out of saving the life of the cow and being in tune with God, but there are many ways he seems disrespectful. You make it sound like the devotee respects *everything*. But as far as I can see, although he really stands up for his Kṛṣṇa conscious opinions, he scorns everything else. I don't see that his respect is universal."

To such arguments the devotee responds: "The Vaiṣṇava's respect is real—not based on fear or diplomacy, like the polite respect businessmen and politicians offer each other. A devotee's respect *is* universal, because he sees everything in connection with Kṛṣṇa. And even though he may speak strongly against the nondevotees on Kṛṣṇa's behalf, he remains humble and naturally respectful toward all. If someone offends Kṛṣṇa, a devotee must object, but that is not disrespectful."

According to *śāstra,* the nondevotee can have no good qualities. Nor should anyone claim respect for his accomplishments in the material world. The devotee respects him as a spirit soul, but not for the bombastic farce of his attainments in this world of illusion. But our saying the devotee respects the president of the United States as much as he respects the ant is not disrespectful of the president. The devotee respects all species because they are spiritual entities. On that account, putting the president on the same level as the ant is a compliment. A devotee doesn't respect only the humans and then kill the animals. And he certainly doesn't respect people for their social position or military strength. If Kṛṣṇa orders the devotee not to respect someone, then the devotee will not dare to offer that person false respect. The devotee is not opinionated. When Kṛṣṇa says the nondevotee is an ass or a rascal (*mūḍhā*), the devotee is in no position to deny it.

The respect the devotee pays to others is in accord with his Kṛṣṇa conscious understanding. His respect is universal, yet he makes distinctions, understanding Kṛṣṇa has given great responsibility to the demigod and an insignificant life to the ant.

In the Tenth Chapter of *Bhagavad-gītā,* we read how all wonderful manifestations—the strength of the strong, the knowledge of the wise, and all beautiful things—come from Kṛṣṇa. It is the Kṛṣṇa-ness in all things that makes the devotee respectful. Therefore the devotee also respects *māyā* as a powerful agent of the Supreme. In the case of *māyā,* however, he offers his respects from a distance.

Although the devotee respects all, he doesn't *worship* anyone except Kṛṣṇa or the pure devotee of Kṛṣṇa. *Worship* is for the Supreme Personality of Godhead alone. But that does not mean that the devotee is disrespectful. If he did not save his exclusive worship for the Supreme Lord, then that would be the greatest disrespect to the Supreme Personality of Godhead.

The topmost devotee, the *mahābhāgavata,* respects even the demons, because he sees everyone in his place as a servant within the plan of the Supreme. But for preaching, the devotee has to distinguish between devotee and demon. And preaching is so important and relishable that sometimes the *mahābhāgavata* comes down to the intermediate position of making distinctions to preach.

In the *Bhagavad-gītā,* Kṛṣṇa teaches us to distinguish between the devotee and the nondevotee and also to see all living entities as His parts and parcels. Kṛṣṇa describes in the Sixteenth Chapter two kinds of people in the world—devotees and nondevotees. But He also says *mamaivāṁśo jīva-loke:* all the *jīvas* are His eternal parts and parcels. He explains as the *jīvas* approach Him, He rewards them accordingly. And His final instruction is that the *jīva* give up all material activities and become His pure devotee.

One who takes up this mission of Kṛṣṇa and preaches is the dearmost servant of the Lord. Although such a devotee may ultimately see that all the *jīvas* are serving the Lord and that, in fact, no one can be against the will of the Lord, still he approaches the nondevotee in humility and tries to offer him Kṛṣṇa consciousness. In a sublime sense, preaching is an offering of deep respect to the nondevotee. The devotee respects the nondevotee as an eternal servant of Kṛṣṇa. Respecting the latent spiritual identity within the heart of the materialist, the devotee encourages everyone to return to their position as loving servants of the Lord. Respect means to appreciate the inherent goodness and superiority of another person, and therefore, preaching to bring out the best in the nondevotee is surely an offering of respect.

In preaching Kṛṣṇa consciousness, a devotee makes distinctions among the different *jīvas*. The scriptures prescribe that a preacher should avoid the demon. Aside from the demon are the innocent nondevotees, and the preacher humbly offers them Kṛṣṇa consciousness. He cannot honestly respect their material position, since they are nondevotees; but he approaches them in humility, feeling himself a lowly servant, to offer them Kṛṣṇa consciousness. In so doing, he may address the nondevotee as advised by Prabhodānanda Sarasvatī: "Oh you are a very learned person and a very admirable gentleman." When addressed in flattering terms, the nondevotee may become inclined to his flatterer. The humble devotee then requests further. "My dear learned sir, although you know so many things already, I please request you to put them aside and hear the philosophy of Lord Caitanya."

A devotee also has relationships with various classes of devotees, and he must also show respect accordingly. *The Nectar of Instruction* states that one should offer mental respect to anyone who is chanting the names of Kṛṣṇa, even if the chanter is not following the regulative principles. This is confirmed in *Caitanya-caritāmṛta, Madhya* 15.106 "Whoever chants the holy name of Kṛṣṇa just once is worshipable and is the topmost human being."

If a devotee finds another devotee who regularly chants the Hare Kṛṣṇa mantra and follows the regulative principles, the devotee considers him his friend. Regular exchanges of love between equal devotees are sharing *prasādam,* offering and receiving gifts, and revealing one's mind. When a devotee meets a very advanced devotee, then he should offer him full respect and treat him as a spiritual master. Discussing these matters in *The Nectar of Instruction,* Śrīla Prabhupāda advises us to know our own position and not imitate advanced devotees.

The Vedic literature is replete with advice on respecting the superior Vaiṣṇava. As stated in *The Nectar of Devotion:* "A person who shows adequate respect to a spiritual master, a *brāhmaṇa,* and an old person is to be understood as being respectful." The disciple offers the spiritual master the same respect as to God, and whatever the spiritual master says, the disciple should try to execute right away. He should give everything he owns to the guru and serve him as a menial servant. If the spiritual master corrects the disciple, he should take the chastisement humbly. The spiritual master will train a sincere disciple to become a compassionate Kṛṣṇa conscious person, so that he too can show respect to all living beings by the welfare work of Kṛṣṇa consciousness.

20
A devotee is without false prestige, *amānī*

False prestige can be considered in two ways: (1) the objects of prestige are falsely prestigious, and (2) our claim to any prestigious object or position is false. A devotee is free of both kinds of false prestige. He is not attracted to the glitter of desirable material possessions, and whatever is attractive he acknowledges as but a reflection of Kṛṣṇa, the all-attractive cause of all causes.

Divisions of quality in the material world—first-class, second-class, third-class—are all false. *Caitanya-caritāmṛta* states that although some material things are considered auspicious and some inauspicious, they are all inauspicious. The folly of making too much over material distinctions is illustrated in the story about a man who appreciated the difference between dry stool and wet stool. Once a man walking on the road observed a pile of stool and pointed it out to his friend. The man commented that the top portion of the stool, which had dried in the sun, was good, whereas the bottom portion, still wet, was bad. But what is the significant difference? Either dry or wet, both are stool.

The illusion of false prestige is so complete that a man identifies his prestigious possession as his very self. The driver of a Rolls Royce thinks he has become a "Rolls man." But even if by riding in his prestigious car he has indeed become a Rolls Royce-quality person, how will that save him from the pinches of fate? Possessing the best credit cards, living in the best neighborhood, having a beautiful wife, the right friends, vacationing in the most exotic places—all these distinctions cannot solve the problems of birth, death, old age, and disease. Kings and queens, Rockefellers and Birlas—all die. Their bodies are buried or burned like anyone else's, and they have to face their karma. Bhaktivinoda Ṭhākura, therefore, declared that the more one makes material progress, the more he becomes an ass.

The word prestige comes from the French: "illusion brought on by magic." The Latin word *praestigiae* has a similar meaning: "juggler's tricks." Magic moments in life—when the actor receives applause, when the writer wins a prize of recognition, when a person meets and conquers his ideal lovemate—all are "juggler's tricks."

You may obtain prestige for a time, but very soon you may also lose it. And you will be very bitter about your loss of prestige. The baseball hero of yesterday makes an error and is booed; last election's winning candidate later suffers ignominy. Kṛṣṇa therefore says in *Bhagavad-gītā* that His dear devotee "is equipoised in honor and dishonor, fame and infamy." According to Bhaktisiddhānta Sarasvatī, fame and material happiness are as valuable as the dung of a boar.

Another kind of false prestige is to take credit for one's achievements. Kṛṣṇa says in *Bhagavad-gītā* that He is ability in man and that intelligence and memory come from Him. Yet even one pursuing transcendental life may falsely claim to be the doer or owner. In the beginning stages, when the false ego is still strong, even the transcendentalist may suffer from this impurity. He may become proud that he is an ascetic, a yogi with powers, a learned devotee-scholar, a worshipful guru, or an ecstatic chanter and dancer. I had a personal experience about undue pride in 1968. I had gone to Boston to open an ISKCON center there one year before, and now I was visiting Śrīla Prabhupāda in New York. I confessed to him that I had the bad mental and verbal habit of trying to take credit for whatever good thing happened in our Boston center. Śrīla Prabhupāda closed his eyes thoughtfully and said, "That feeling you have, that 'I am something' is not wrong. But you have to know who you are. When you come to the point of thinking that 'I am the servant of Kṛṣṇa' then the ego is all right."

The servant of the servant of God has, by the grace of guru and Kṛṣṇa, gained that which is actually admirable and influential. He has become a confidential associate of the Supreme Personality of Godhead. To associate with genuine devotees, to work as a disciple of an *ācārya* in disciplic succession, to be allowed to live in Kṛṣṇa's temple and serve the Deity, to be engaged in the highest welfare work for humanity—all are really admirable assets. But a pure devotee, while considering such assets a great privilege, knows they are all the mercy of Kṛṣṇa and not something he has earned simply by his hard work or personal success. Even the smallest act in devotional service, such as polishing the brass objects on the Lord's altar, is more significant than any prestigious, nondevotional act, because by polishing the Lord's paraphernalia, a devotee can please the Supreme Personality of Godhead. When Kṛṣṇa is pleased, the whole universe is pleased, and the devotee becomes honored among saintly people throughout the three material worlds and the spiritual world as well.

When a devotee loses all false prestige and becomes completely absorbed in humble service at the lotus feet of Kṛṣṇa, he becomes eligible to go to Kṛṣṇa and associate with Him in eternity, bliss, and knowledge. The aspiring devotee fights hard to kick off all vestiges of false prestige, and he prays to Kṛṣṇa: "O savior of the fallen, please don't kick me away, but allow me to serve Your servants. I am a rascal possessed by material desires and am falsely taking credit for things which are Yours, not mine. Please deliver me."

21

A devotee is grave, *gambhīra.*

The Nectar of Devotion states:

> A person who does not express his mind to everyone, or whose mental activity and plan of action are very difficult to understand, is called grave. After Lord Śrī Kṛṣṇa had been offended by Brahmā, Brahmā prayed to Him to be excused. But in spite of his offering nice prayers to Kṛṣṇa, Brahmā could not understand whether Kṛṣṇa was satisfied or still dissatisfied. In other words, Kṛṣṇa was so grave that He did not take the prayers of Brahmā very seriously. Another instance of Kṛṣṇa's gravity is found in connection with His love affairs with Rādhārāṇī. Kṛṣṇa was always very silent about His love affairs with Rādhārāṇī, so much that Baladeva, Kṛṣṇa's elder brother and constant companion, could not understand the transformations of Kṛṣṇa on account of His gravity.

A devotee's emotions and concentration are not swept away because the next person is giddy or morose. He doesn't feel obliged to immediately turn from his meditation on Kṛṣṇa to talking nonsense, just because the next person would like to talk nonsense. Although he is not antisocial, first and foremost he must always remember Kṛṣṇa. That is the prime rule: always remember Kṛṣṇa and never forget Kṛṣṇa. A devotee thinks that if he is at all to help another person, then he can only do so when he is himself centered on Kṛṣṇa.

In *Śrīmad-Bhāgavatam,* in the conversation between Kardama Muni and Svāyambhuva Manu, we find an example of the Vaiṣṇava's gravity. Svāyambhuva Manu, the emperor, had come to the cottage of Kardama to ask the sage to marry his daughter. The sage agreed on the condition that, after giving her a child, he would take *sannyāsa* according to the will of Lord Viṣṇu. Kardama then became silent and, thinking of Lord Viṣṇu, smiled.

> It appears that Kardama Muni was fully absorbed in Kṛṣṇa consciousness because as soon as he became silent, he at once began to think of Lord Viṣṇu. That is the way of Kṛṣṇa consciousness. Pure devotees are so absorbed in thought of Kṛṣṇa that they have no other engagement; although they may seem to think or act otherwise, they are always thinking of Kṛṣṇa. The smile of such a Kṛṣṇa conscious person is so attractive that simply by smiling he wins so many admirers, disciples and followers.
>
> —*Bhāg*. 3.22.21, purport

Once, as Śrīla Prabhupāda was arriving at an Australian airport, a woman reporter asked him, "When you got off the plane you looked very grave. Why is that?" Śrīla Prabhupāda replied that he was always thinking of Kṛṣṇa, the Supreme Personality of Godhead, and since Kṛṣṇa is so great, "naturally we become grave." The reporter then asked Prabhupāda if he ever smiled. In reply Prabhupāda smiled, thus assuring us not only that he could smile but that he was still thinking of Kṛṣṇa.

Regarding Kṛṣṇa's gravity, a verse in *Śrīmad-Bhāgavatam* describes the Kumara's bewilderment at hearing the profound speeches from the mouth of Lord Viṣṇu in Vaikuṇṭha:

> The Lord's excellent speech was difficult to comprehend because of its momentous import and its most profound significance. The sages heard it with wide open ears and pondered it as well. But although hearing, they could not understand what He intended to do.
>
> PURPORT
>
> It should be understood that no one can surpass the Supreme Personality of Godhead in speaking. There is no difference between the Supreme Person and His speeches, for He stands on the absolute platform. The sages tried with wide open ears to understand the words from the lips of the Supreme Lord, but although His speech was very concise and meaningful, the sages could not completely comprehend what He was saying. They could not even comprehend the purport of the speech or what the Supreme Lord wanted to do. Nor could they understand whether the Lord was angry or pleased with them.
>
> —*Bhāg* 3.16.14 and purport

If one hears the profound speeches of the Supreme Personality of Godhead, one becomes grave. Similarly, if one associates with serious devotees, he too becomes serious and grave. There are many light moments in Kṛṣṇa consciousness, but for the conditioned soul to give up his material life and prepare himself to go back to Godhead is no joke. It is a very deep purpose. And when, by chanting and hearing, a devotee realizes something of the holy name and *Śrīmad-Bhāgavatam,* then his philosophic outlook deepens more and more.

22

A devotee is compassionate, *karuṇa*.

The Nectar of Devotion describes compassion:

A person who is unable to bear another's distress is called compassionate.

Kṛṣṇa's compassion for distressed persons was exhibited when He released all of the kings imprisoned by Magadhendra. While dying, Grandfather Bhīṣma prayed to Kṛṣṇa and described Him as the sun which eradicated darkness. The kings who were imprisoned by Magadhendra were put into dark cells, and when Kṛṣṇa appeared there, the darkness immediately disappeared, just as if the sun had risen. In other words, although Magadhendra was able to imprison so many kings, upon the appearance of Kṛṣṇa they were all released. Kṛṣṇa did this Out of His sincere compassion for the kings.

Kṛṣṇa's compassion was also exhibited when Grandfather Bhīṣma was lying on the bed of arrows which had been shot through his body. While lying in this position, Bhīṣma was very anxious to see Kṛṣṇa, and thus Kṛṣṇa appeared there. Upon seeing the pitiable condition of Bhīṣma, Kṛṣṇa began speaking with tears in His eyes. Not only was He shedding tears, but He also forgot Himself in His compassion. Therefore, instead of offering obeisances to Kṛṣṇa directly, devotees offer obeisances to His compassionate nature.

> Actually, because Kṛṣṇa is the Supreme Personality of Godhead, it is very difficult to approach Him. But the devotees, taking advantage of His compassionate nature, which is represented by Rādhārāṇī, always pray to Rādhārāṇī for Kṛṣṇa's compassion.

Kṛpalu (merciful), *vadānya* (magnanimous), and *sarvopakāraka* (working for the welfare of everyone), are all similar to *karuṇa,* compassion. As we near the end of our praise of the twenty-six qualities of a devotee, we must again appreciate that the devotees are workers on behalf of those who are suffering. The good qualities of the devotees are meant to serve others. The above quote from *The Nectar of Devotion* describes Rādhārāṇī as the protectress of devotional service and of all devotees who want to approach the Lord. She is compassionate. Rādhārāṇī, like all genuine devotees, wants to help others become devotees of Kṛṣṇa. We, therefore, see these traits repeated more than any other qualities of the devotee—mercy, magnanimity, welfare work, compassion. Lord Caitanya Mahāprabhu and also our spiritual master, Śrīla Prabhupāda, taught these qualities. And for practically doing the compassionate work of the Kṛṣṇa consciousness movement, Śrīla Prabhupāda gave us four aphorisms: (1) preaching is the essence, (2) purity is the force, (3) books are the basis, and (4) utility is the principle.

The essence of compassion is preaching. But the force that drives the preaching is purity. Preaching rests on the sincere, pure hearts and minds of the devotees. When a devotee surrenders to Kṛṣṇa, Kṛṣṇa blesses his efforts. At that time we say a devotee is empowered to preach. Preaching is not just a matter of getting a devotee to appear on television with a big personality or pushing a devotee beside a world-famous person so the press will take his photo and put it in the newspaper. The devotee going to preach must actually be pure.

Purity is not an abstract thing. A pure devotee must chant sixteen rounds a day, he must avoid the four kinds of sinful activities, and he must dedicate his life and soul to the spiritual master and the Kṛṣṇa consciousness movement. Wherever a pure devotee goes, he will be well received by persons interested in real spiritual life. If he is not pure, however, if he has some mixed motive of sense gratification, then even if he appears in the newspaper, he will not be able to move people to Kṛṣṇa consciousness.

When we say "books are the basis," we mean Śrīla Prabhupāda's books. Śrīla Prabhupāda was empowered by his full surrender to his spiritual master and Kṛṣṇa to compose almost sixty full-size books—translations and commentaries on the Vedic literature. Śrīla Prabhupāda's books are not just translations; they are transcendental literature to guide a whole world of devotees for the next ten thousand years. According to the Vedic calendar, although it is now Kali-yuga, Kṛṣṇa consciousness can spread very effectively over the next ten thousand years. The law, art, politics, science, philosophy, and sociology of that Kṛṣṇa conscious era are all contained in Śrīla Prabhupāda's books. Everything is there, because Kṛṣṇa is there. Śrīla Prabhupāda repeatedly advised all his followers to carefully read his books again and again, because one can become Kṛṣṇa conscious just by reading these books. The *Skanda Purāṇa* states, "A person who is constantly engaged in reading literature enunciating the cultivation of Vaiṣṇava devotional service is always glorious in human society, and certainly Lord Kṛṣṇa becomes pleased with him. A person who very carefully keeps such literature at home and offers respectful obeisances to it becomes freed from all sinful reactions and ultimately becomes worshipable by the demigods."

Although those practicing devotional service will especially appreciate Śrīla Prabhupāda's books, their value to one who has never heard about Kṛṣṇa is incalculable. The conditioned soul, in complete ignorance of his future, is headed for doom, like a log headed downstream towards the waterfall. But by reading *Śrīmad-Bhāgavatam,* a conditioned soul can be saved from his fate of repeated birth and death, just as a log sometimes goes ashore and is saved from crashing over the falls.

The best compassionate work is to take part in printing and distributing these Kṛṣṇa conscious literatures in different languages all over the world. Śrīla Prabhupāda said history will one day tell that these books saved the world. At present they are not fully appreciated, and this is because Kṛṣṇa is not yet appreciated. The ordinary human being misspends his life from boyhood through old age in foolish activities without inquiry into God. But it is the plan of Kṛṣṇa that He will become more and more manifest in this world within the next ten thousand years—through Śrīla Prabhupāda's books. When five thousand years ago the sages at Naimisāraṇya asked how a conditioned soul could contact Kṛṣṇa since He had left the planet and Kali-yuga had begun, Sūta Gosvāmī replied that Kṛṣṇa was now present:

kṛṣṇe sva-dhāmopagate
dharma-jñānādibhiḥ saha
kalau naṣṭa-dṛśām eṣa
purāṇārko 'dhunoditaḥ

> This *Bhāgavata Purāṇa* is as brilliant as the sun, and it has arisen just after the departure of Lord Kṛṣṇa to His own abode, accompanied by religion, knowledge, etc. Persons who have lost their vision due to the dense darkness of ignorance in the age of Kali shall get light from this *Purāṇa*.
>
> —*Bhāg*. 1.3.43

The aphorism "utility is the principle" refers to using material things in the service of Kṛṣṇa. When a devotee realizes that he can spread Kṛṣṇa consciousness in every country, adjusting things according to time, place, and circumstances—but without changing the *paramparā*—then he becomes enlivened and enlightened further in how to spread Kṛṣṇa consciousness. According to his devotion, Kṛṣṇa gives him the intelligence to preach in a practical way. The jurisdiction of Kṛṣṇa consciousness has no boundaries, and the Kṛṣṇa conscious preacher who realizes this is the greatest renunciant.

Following the spirit of Śrīla Prabhupāda's four aphorisms, the workers of the Kṛṣṇa consciousness movement can become compassionate to everyone. The quality of compassion is not reserved only for a few rare saints. Rather, sainthood is now, by Lord Caitanya's mercy, open to all who submissively hear and take up the *saṅkīrtana* movement.

23

A devotee is a friend, *maitra*.

A devotee is a friend because he directs you to Kṛṣṇa. Kṛṣṇa is the best friend of all living entities. I may be your friend, but even if I have the best intentions, I will leave you after some years, whether by destiny, disagreement, or death. I may be your friend yet be unable to understand you or to help you; and certainly at the time of death I cannot save you, because I cannot save even myself. But I *can* be a true friend by reminding you to chant Hare Kṛṣṇa.

Although the devotee, by virtue of his pointing us to Kṛṣṇa, is a friend, his friendly act is not merely formal, like a traffic policeman giving you directions. The devotee-friend has all the virtues of a friend in the truest sense of friendship. Devotees live together, chant, share, and solace each other in spiritual intimacy. Because there is no sense gratification in Kṛṣṇa consciousness, devotees don't spoil their friendship with ulterior motives. In *Bhagavad-gītā* 10.9 Kṛṣṇa describes the association of devotees, "The thoughts of My pure devotees dwell in Me, their lives are fully devoted to My service, and they derive great satisfaction and bliss enlightening one another and conversing about Me."

Narottama dāsa Ṭhākura says, "I am always hankering for the association of Rāmacandra [his Godbrother]."

In the pastimes of Lord Caitanya, devotees like Rūpa Gosvāmī and Haridāsa Ṭhākura were fast friends because of their like mentalities. The Six Gosvāmīs also regularly associated together sharing their Kṛṣṇa conscious realizations, singing *bhajana,* and taking *prasādam.*

Important to any friendship is that the friends stay together, even in difficulty. Devotees do this. They worship Kṛṣṇa together, work together, go out chanting Hare Kṛṣṇa together; sometimes they are even forced to go to jail together. And sometimes they come together before their spiritual master and share their intimate progress in spiritual life. Even if they are not appreciated by others, it is a fact that they are the friends of all the conditioned souls.

Certain sensitive thinkers have noted that an important part of human friendship is that one friend supports and encourages the solitude of the other. But only a devotee really knows how to nourish another's solitude. In Kṛṣṇa consciousness solitude does not refer to mere egoism in a void. In the positive sense, solitude means an individual's eternal relationship with Kṛṣṇa. A friend can respect another person's individual relationship with Kṛṣṇa and try to encourage it. Protecting another's solitude does not mean simply to leave him alone but to know, as a friend, that when your friend is alone he is actually with Kṛṣṇa. Friends in Kṛṣṇa consciousness help each other like pilots on the ground before take-off. They share their experiences and strategies because when they are aloft in their planes, one pilot cannot help another. Taking off alone in a plane is a metaphor to describe the spirit soul's solitary passage after death. At that time each person has to face the result of his own individual karma. But if he has spent his time well in Kṛṣṇa conscious association, he will have grasped the essence of remembering Kṛṣṇa and be able to go home, back to Godhead, at the time of death. Friendship in Kṛṣṇa consciousness is, therefore, eternal because all pure devotees finally meet at the destination in the spiritual world.

24

A devotee is a poet, *kavi*.

In *Caitanya-caritāmṛta,* Rāmananda Rāya praises the wonderful poetic descriptions by Rūpa Gosvāmī:

> "'What is the use of a bowman's arrow or a poet's poetry if they penetrate the heart but do not cause the head to spin?'
>
> "Without Your mercy, such poetic expressions would be impossible for an ordinary living being to write. My guess is that You have given him the power."
>
> Śrī Caitanya Mahāprabhu replied, "I met Śrīla Rūpa Gosvāmī at Prayāg. He attracted and satisfied Me because of his qualities."
>
> Śrī Caitanya Mahāprabhu praised the metaphors and other literary ornaments of Śrīla Rūpa Gosvāmī's transcendental poetry. Without such poetic attributes, He said, there is no possibility of preaching transcendental mellows.
>
> —Cc. *Antya* 1.195–98

It appears from the statements of Lord Caitanya that unless a person can think in poetic metaphors, he cannot appreciate Kṛṣṇa in His eternal *rasas.* One of the many names for Kṛṣṇa is *uttamāśloka,* which means that He is praised with the choicest poetic words. To describe the beauty of Kṛṣṇa's form, His pastimes, the nectar of His holy name, the glories of His abode, Vṛndāvana, and the sweetness of His love, is impossible—except by poetic language.

The compilers of the *śāstra*, such as Śrīla Vyāsadeva and in the later age Kṛṣṇadāsa Kavirāja, were all highly endowed poets. The *śāstras* compare Kṛṣṇa's hue to the fresh raincloud, His eyes to lotuses, the rays from His toenails to soothing autumnal moons. When Lord Caitanya says that without poetic metaphors a devotee cannot describe Kṛṣṇa's pastimes, this does not mean that Kṛṣṇa is imaginary or unreal. Rather, Kṛṣṇa consciousness is not dull; it requires poetry.

Kṛṣṇa's qualities demand to be described in the choicest poetic words, and the pure devotee is equal to the task, because Kṛṣṇa empowers him. After Sanātana Gosvāmī received full instructions from Lord Caitanya, he prayed to be blessed with inspiration to write everything down:

> If You want to make a lame man like me dance, kindly bestow Your transcendental blessings by keeping Your lotus feet on my head.
>
> Now, will you please tell me, "Let whatever I have instructed all be fully manifest unto you." By benedicting me in this way, You will give me strength to describe all this.
>
> —Cc. *Madhya* 23.122

Many references state that only authorized devotees can write transcendental literatures, whether poetry or prose. To be able to write *paramparā* descriptions of Kṛṣṇa is a prerogative of the devotee who has been blessed by Kṛṣṇa and guru. The empowered *kavi* never takes credit for himself but acknowledges that whatever he writes is dictated by the Lord in the heart. A devotee should, therefore, never write anything speculative. Whatever he writes should be first confirmed by Kṛṣṇa and the Vaiṣṇavas. He should write only on the order of higher authorities in Kṛṣṇa consciousness. There is no scope for a devotee's becoming an ambitious poet or author, famous for his own compositions. Kṛṣṇadāsa Kavirāja explains that his motive in writing is to purify himself and to bless the world with the pastimes of Lord Caitanya.

The compilers of the *śāstra*s are not ordinary human beings, and the *śāstra*s are not their own writings but were dictated by Kṛṣṇa Himself. Śrīla Vyāsadeva, the compiler of the Vedas, and Vālmīkī, the author of the Ra*māyā*na, saw the Supreme Lord in their meditations, and their intelligences were directed unerringly to compose perfect Sanskrit *ślokas*. Only five hundred years ago Rūpa and Sanātana Gosvāmīs entered directly into the pastimes of Rādhā and Kṛṣṇa and described them in their poems and plays. Their Sanskrit writings display expertise in grammar, logic, and metaphor. Lord Caitanya Himself demonstrated mastery in the art of literary criticism by defeating Keśava Kāshmīri in Navadvīpa. Lord Caitanya found defects in the renowned poet's compositions by intricately applying various rules of Sanskrit grammar composition. Jīva Gosvāmī is another highly-acclaimed Sanskritist whose Vaiṣṇava philosophical dissertations are profound and poetic. *Kavi* means "learned" as well as "poetic" and Jīva Gosvāmī is both.

Not all the Vaiṣṇava poets in disciplic succession wrote in highly literate Sanskrit mantras. Narottama dāsa Ṭhākura composed his songs in simple Bengali language, but the erudite Vedic *ācārya* Viśvanātha Cakravartī Ṭhākura later approved the songs of Narottama dāsa to be as good as Vedic mantras.

The essence of Vaiṣṇava poetry, therefore, is devotion to Kṛṣṇa. It is not the language itself that is important, but the subject matter. An example of this is in Kṛṣṇa's appreciation of the praises of the ladies of Hastināpura who witnessed His departure for Dvārakā:

> Absorbed in the thought of the transcendental qualities of the Lord, who was sung in select poetry, the ladies on the roofs of all the houses of Hastināpura began to talk of Him. This talk was more attractive than the hymns of the Vedas.
>
> PURPORT
>
> Anything sung in the praise of the Lord is *śruti-mantra*. . . . The Vedic hymns in the *Upaniṣads* are sometimes indirectly directed to the Supreme Lord. But the talks of the ladies were directly spoken of the Lord, and thus they were more pleasing to the heart. The ladies' talks appeared to be more valuable than the learned *brāhmaṇas'* benedictions.
>
> —*Bhāg*. 1.10.20

The American poet Allen Ginsberg met Śrīla Prabhupāda on a number of occasions, and on one occasion Śrīla Prabhupāda encouraged him to write poems about Kṛṣṇa. Allen said he didn't want to restrict himself to the single image of Kṛṣṇa. Abandoning Kṛṣṇa, the Absolute Truth, such poets throw themselves into the world of illusion. They do not know that everything is Kṛṣṇa and that they simply lack the vision to see everything within Him. Kṛṣṇa is everything. He is the whole universe, including every person, every soul, every tree, every flower, all life—the beginning, middle, end, and beyond. There cannot be any question of Kṛṣṇa's being a limited image. Poetry without reference to Kṛṣṇa is "decoration of a dead body." At a funeral the dead body may be dressed in a tuxedo or a gown, but it is still a useless corpse. Similarly, the expert and inventive methods of composition used by the poets throughout the ages may be a testimony of their dedication to the language and to their urge for evocation, but because they have missed the central point, Kṛṣṇa, their words, no matter how expertly composed, remain "decorations of a dead body." No one can benefit by reading the writings of unrealized souls, who invent their own meaning of existence. No one was ever liberated by such poetry.

Aside from making poetic compositions, a devotee is a poet by his poetic perception. He is not dull. He tastes Kṛṣṇa in pure water and sees the sun as Kṛṣṇa's eye. He uses language to describe God. He has in his mind's eye a vision of intense beauty, the transcendental form of Śrī Kṛṣṇa, the Supreme Personality of Godhead. He frees his own life from the fetters of what mundaners call reality and dedicates himself to serving the Supreme Absolute. Always hearing transcendental sounds passed down from great poets of the past, always chanting the Hare Kṛṣṇa mantra, dancing and singing in ecstasy, and aspiring to please Kṛṣṇa, the devotee lives minute to minute in ever-fresh Kṛṣṇa consciousness. He is a poet.

25

A devotee is expert, *dakṣa.*

Devotees utilize many skills in Kṛṣṇa consciousness. The book Kṛṣṇa, describes the skills Kṛṣṇa learned at the *gurukula* of Sandīpanī Muni. For Kṛṣṇa's service a devotee may occasionally take courses or study a skill—how to use a computer or printing press. But more often devotees learn "on the job" how to become expert for Kṛṣṇa. A skill can be learned by practice, and more importantly, Kṛṣṇa, being in the heart of the devotee, can teach him whatever is required. Kṛṣṇa actually teaches everyone, because it is He who supplies memory and intelligence. But in the case of the devotees, He promises, "I give the intelligence by which they can come to Me." We therefore see devotees applying their skills in constructing temples, learning arts and crafts, dealing in business, cooking, painting, and so on. But devotees are not the only persons who are expert in these matters. In fact, many nondevotees are more expert in these skills. A devotee's being expert, therefore, cannot refer merely to his executing certain manual and intellectual skills in the service of Kṛṣṇa.

The real expertise of the pure devotee is that he is able to extricate himself and others from the difficult web of *māyā*. The conditioned soul is imprisoned in the material world under the divine energy of Kṛṣṇa (*mama māyā duratyayā*), and the material universe itself is covered with many layers of material elements: earth, water, fire, air, etc., each many thousands of miles broad. The deluding energy, *māyā*, is herself very expert, keeping the conditioned souls illusioned and bound. *Śrīmad-Bhāgavatam* compares the materialistic householder to a silkworm who has spun a cocoon around himself and become inextricably entangled. He who becomes free of *māyā*, free of the cycle of birth and death, is expert.

The supreme expert is Kṛṣṇa, and it is He who gives us the expert process of devotional service. *Dharmān tu sākṣāt-bhagavat-praṇītam*: no one can enunciate true religion except the Supreme Lord Himself. Lord Kṛṣṇa in His munificent form as Lord Caitanya gave the method whereby even the most fallen and slowest souls of Kali-yuga could revive their pure Kṛṣṇa consciousness—"chant Hare Kṛṣṇa." Lord Caitanya knew that in this age people would not be able to practice severe austerities or understand Vedanta through meditation or Sanskrit. Therefore He very expertly gave us the *mahā-mantra* and simple process of hearing *Śrīmad-Bhāgavatam* and *Bhagavad-gītā* from pure devotees in disciplic succession.

For us the required expertise is simple: we have to grasp the lotus feet of Lord Caitanya's Kṛṣṇa conscious practices. Millions of species of life and millions of varieties of sense gratification are being offered to the bewildered conditioned soul. Moreover, especially in the present age, one's chances of becoming free from *māyā* are more and more reduced. Maya's influence has expanded, and even if a person is inclined to spiritual life, a bogus guru is very likely to cheat him. We are, therefore, not playing with words when we take the meaning of *expert* to be, "He who becomes free from *māyā* by surrendering to Kṛṣṇa." Such an expert devotee avoids the greatest danger, and he attains the greatest goal. Who is more worthy of the name *expert*?

Finding the ways and means to preach Kṛṣṇa consciousness and thus extricate others from *māyā*'s entanglement is another expertise of the devotee. When Lord Caitanya began His *saṅkīrtana* movement, He had to figure out a way to reach those who were very reluctant. So that people would respect Him, He decided to take the *sannyāsa* order.

Śrīla Prabhupāda also, as the first Vaiṣṇava to preach in the West, had to employ expert methods according to time and place. We have already mentioned under the quality of *magnanimous* how Śrīla Prabhupāda arranged marriages for his disciples and made other adjustments in his Kṛṣṇa consciousness movement. His expertise was that he made Kṛṣṇa consciousness lenient without compromising any of its principles. An empowered pure devotee like Śrīla Prabhupāda takes on great responsibilities and anxieties in thinking how to spread Kṛṣṇa consciousness. Day and night he concerns himself with managing the Kṛṣṇa consciousness movement and taking care of neophyte devotees. Yet he does not take credit for his successes nor blame Kṛṣṇa for any failures. But when Kṛṣṇa sees His pure devotee's anxiety to preach, He helps him. The best expertise of the devotee is sincere surrender. If Lord Kṛṣṇa takes charge of our affairs, then certainly we are in expert bands. We should diligently learn the art of surrender to Kṛṣṇa and apply it purely.

I have heard Śrīla Prabhupāda explain the quality of *expert* in yet another way. He said, "A devotee is expert. This means that he is willing to do anything. He does not say because he is a *brāhmaṇa* he cannot do a menial task." Again, this meaning of expert implies surrender.

By this definition Śrīla Prabhupāda was encouraging us to engage in whatever task had to be done in Kṛṣṇa consciousness. The ability to surrender and do the needful is the sign of an expert devotee. We often think of an expert in a narrow sense as a specialist, but in devotional service we may find the expert cleaning the bathroom, polishing the *kāratalas,* or washing his clothes. Expertise in skills will not get us back to Godhead, but rather the expertise in seeing our real position as the servant of the servant of the Lord.

Surely Śrīla Prabhupāda was one of the most expert Vaiṣṇavas in every sense. And he urged us, "Become expert." We also must learn how to deliver Kṛṣṇa to the "expert" avoiders of His mercy. We also must figure out the ways and means. There is no alternative. Kṛṣṇa will not be pleased if we remain inept. We must also learn to be expert.

26

A devotee is silent, *maunī.*

A devotee never speaks any nonsense; this is his silence. *Maunī* does not refer to vows of not speaking or becoming incommunicado, as is practiced by some yogis. Of course, if a person doesn't know Kṛṣṇa, then better he be silent. Sometimes, therefore, a guru will ask a frivolous disciple whose speech is uncontrolled to practice complete *mauna.*

Speech is very important. A fool is not exposed until he begins to speak. As with a naughty child, it is better for an impersonalist meditator to be completely quiet. But if he can say something in the service of Kṛṣṇa, then better he speak.

The devotee can speak the glories of Kṛṣṇa and present the philosophy of Kṛṣṇa consciousness all day long. A devotee wants to always chant Hare Kṛṣṇa, Hare Kṛṣṇa, Kṛṣṇa Kṛṣṇa, Hare Hare/ Hare Rāma, Hare Rāma, Rāma Rāma, Hare Hare. Why should he be silent? He has such great love for Śrī Kṛṣṇa that he wants to tell everyone about Him. His Divine Grace Śrīla Prabhupāda would constantly preach, whether to large audiences, to small groups of devotees, or even when alone with his servant. He loved to talk about Kṛṣṇa; he never tired. And he never varied from the Absolute. Yet Prabhupāda was perfectly silent in that he spoke only the conclusion of Kṛṣṇa consciousness.

Sometimes Śrīla Prabhupāda wouldn't speak at all. I rode with him on a long jet flight from Frankfurt to Melbourne, and he spoke only a few times. Most of the time he read or chanted silently on his beads.

I once asked Śrīla Prabhupāda a question about the silence of a devotee in a puzzling passage I found in the Kṛṣṇa book: "Sometimes in autumn the falls come down from the top of the hill to supply clean water, and sometimes they stop. Similarly, sometimes great saintly persons distribute clear knowledge, and sometimes they are silent." On a morning walk at Juhu Beach in Bombay I asked Prabhupāda about this passage. "What does it mean," I asked, "that the devotee sometimes speaks and sometimes is silent?"

Śrīla Prabhupāda replied, "It means he is not obliged." I took this to be part of the pure devotee's gravity. Certainly he is always inclined to talk about Kṛṣṇa, but if, for example, some foolish person wants him to reveal the confidential pastimes of Kṛṣṇa or to take advantage of him in some way, he is not obliged. That might be an occasion calling for a devotee's silence. At other times the devotee may be in an ecstatic mood where he is unable to speak. Or someone may make such a foolish proposal to him that the most telling reply is silence itself. I remember a boy repeatedly asking Prabhupāda to talk about how it felt to be in separation from his spiritual master, Bhaktisiddhānta Sarasvatī. Prabhupāda was repeatedly silent to the request, and finally said, "This is not required," meaning he would not speak about it.

Another example of a great devotee's using silence is that of Lord Caitanya silently listening to Sārvabhauma Bhaṭṭācārya speak Vedanta philosophy for seven days. Sārvabhauma finally became frustrated and asked why

Lord Caitanya was silent. Sārvabhauma said that if Lord Caitanya had some questions at least He could ask them, or if He disagreed He could say. But why was He silent? In this way Lord Caitanya showed His respect to the great scholar, and at the same time dramatically showed His disapproval. When Lord Caitanya finally spoke, He defeated all the Māyāvādī ideas Sārvabhauma had been expounding for seven days. Lord Caitanya's silence was also a demonstration of tolerance.

Śrīla Prabhupāda once told some of us in his room that at night when we took rest, we should silently think over all that we had said during the day.

So there are some varied uses for silence in Kṛṣṇa consciousness, but the main purport is that a devotee is silent in nonsense, but always eager to talk about Kṛṣṇa.

* * *

When actually manifested in life, the qualities of a genuine devotee are as deep as the fathomless ocean. Coming in touch with a pure devotee and seeing his manifestation of a single quality, such as mercifulness or silence, can move one to a worshipful appreciation. It is not possible to fully describe the essence of these qualities in the lives of the pure devotees. As I try to write of these qualities I feel my own lacking. These descriptions of the twenty-six qualities should not be taken as exhaustive; rather, I am just trying to make a few valid observations in accordance with the conclusions of the *śāstras*. I hope this will impel others to further appreciate devotees and devotional qualities.

ACKNOWLEDMENTS

I would like to thank the following disciples and friends who helped reprint this book:

Madana-mohana dāsa, Mādhava dāsa, Nancy Dutra, Rādhā-Ramana dāsa, Sankirtana dāsa.

Special thanks to Śāstra dāsa for his kind donation to reprint this book.

His Divine Grace A. C. Bhaktivedanta Swami Prabhupāda lived in this world from 1896 to 1977. Born in Calcutta, India, he first met his spiritual master, Śrīla Bhaktisiddhānta Sarasvatī Gosvāmī, in 1922. At their first meeting he was asked to spread the Vedic knowledge all over the world, and during his many years as a married businessman, he often contemplated this order of his spiritual master. At the age of 63, he accepted the renounced order of life (*sannyāsa*) to help fulfill this mission. From his humble surroundings at the Rādhā-Dāmodara temple in Vṛndāvana, he began work on his life's masterpiece: a multivolume English translation of the eighteen-thousand-verse *Śrīmad-Bhāgavatam* complete with elaborate commentary.

In 1965, with 40 rupees in his pocket, he came by freighter from India to New York City. After almost a year of great difficulty and heroic perseverance, he established the International Society for Krishna Consciousness. In the twelve short years before he passed away, he had guided the Society and watched it grow to a worldwide society of more than one hundred āśramas, schools, temples, institutes, cultural centers, and farm communities.

In Śrīla Prabhupāda's own view, his most significant contribution is his books. Highly respected by scholars for their authority, depth, and clarity, they are used as textbooks in numerous college courses. His writings have been translated into over fifty languages. Despite his advanced age, Śrīla Prabhupāda circled the globe fourteen times on lecture tours that took him to six continents. Yet this vigorous schedule did not slow his prolific literary output. His writings constitute a veritable library of Vedic philosophy, religion, literature, and culture.

For more information about Śrīla Prabhupāda and his work, please visit www. harekrishna.com, or contact Bhaktivedanta Book Trust, P. O. Box 34074, Los Angeles, CA 90034, Phone: 1-310-837-5283, FAX: 1-310-837-1056.

Satsvarūpa dāsa Goswami is a Vaiṣṇava writer, poet, and artist. He was among the first young Americans to assist Śrīla Prabhupāda with his mission in the West and, as Śrīla Prabhupāda's intimate disciple, he served as personal secretary for many years. He is also the author of Śrīla Prabhupāda's authorized biography, *Śrīla Prabhupāda-līlāmṛta.* While traveling, lecturing on Kṛṣṇa consciousness, and instructing disciples worldwide, he has published many books including poems, memoirs, essays, novels, and studies based on the Vaiṣṇava scriptures. In recent years, his devotional life has evolved to include the creation of numerous paintings, drawings, and sculptures that lovingly capture and express the artist's absorption in the culture of Kṛṣṇa consciousness.

For more information about Satsvarūpa dāsa Goswami and his work, please visit Gītā-nagarī Press at www.gnpress.org or contact P. O. Box 445, La Crosse, Florida 32658, 1-877-295-8942.

Other books by Satsvarūpa dāsa Goswami

Prabhupāda Meditations

Life with the Perfect Master
Prabhupāda Nectar
Calling Out to Śrīla Prabhupāda/Poems and Prayers
He Lives Forever
My Letters from Śrīla Prabhupāda (Volumes 1–3)
Prabhupāda Appreciation
Prabhupāda-līlā

Living with the Scriptures

Qualities of Śrī Kṛṣṇa
Saints and Sages of Ancient India
Cc. Āśraya
Living with the Scriptures
Nīti-śāstra: Sayings of Cāṇakya
Spiritualized Dictionary
A Poor Man Read's the Bhāgavatam

Devotional Practices

Entering the Life of Prayer
Japa Reform Notebook
Vaiṣṇava Behavior/ 26 Qualities of a Devotee
Vaisnava Compassion

Devotional Practices (continued)

Begging for the Nectar of the Holy Name
Reading Reform
Truthfulness, The Last Leg of Religion

New Writings

Every Day, Just Write
When the Saints Come Marching In
Sanatorium
Under Dark Stars

Devotional Writings

Shack Notes
Passing Places, Eternal Truths
Photo Preaching

Poetry

Can a White Man be a Haribol
From Matter to Spirit
Gentle Power
Given Time
Prose-poetry at Castlegregory, Ireland
Stowies
The Waves at Jagannātha Purī
The Worshipable Deity and Other Poems (1984)
Writing in Gratitude